CONCILIUM

concilium 1999/1

UNANSWERED QUESTIONS

Edited by

Christoph Theobald and
Dietmar Mieth

SCM Press · London
Orbis Books · Maryknoll

Published by SCM Press, 9–17 St Albans Place, London N1
and by Orbis Books, Maryknoll, NY 10545

Copyright © Stichting Concilium

English translations © 1999 SCM-Canterbury Press Ltd and Orbis Books,
Maryknoll

ISBN: 0 334 03052 8 (UK)
ISBN: 1 57075 225 7 (USA)

Typeset at The Spartan Press Ltd, Lymington, Hants
Printed by Biddles Ltd, Guildford and King's Lynn

Concilium Published February, April, June, October, December.

Contents

Editorial

The Second Vatican Council was a council of transition. It met in full awareness that very soon not only would new questions arise but, precisely because of its open method (a pastoral form of doctrine, signs of the times, and so on), new models and new ways of proceeding would have to be found. In fact the reception of the Council took place in two directions. The 'official reception' continued to be based on the classic distinction between doctrine and discipline in order to work progressively towards an integration of the new (Vatican II) into the Old (Trent and Vatican I). But at the same time the 'practical reception' at the grass roots brought out new problems with a whole set of experiences and experiments opening up new solutions. The eventful history of *Concilium*, founded thirty-five years ago, is a reflection of this process and all its tensions, a process in which it has become increasingly different to articulate the historical and cultural differentiations of context and the normative structure of the Christian tradition.

In the first issue of 1999, we shall touch on the problem of method and bring together a number of questions which in this pivotal period are at the heart of the ecclesiastical debate, since they have proved to be symptomatic of more global and more fundamental orientations in the church. Obviously, we have to be selective, but we have made sure that key issues have not been omitted. We shall not be touching on topics which will be dealt with in other issues of 1999 (frontier violations, new identities, the non-ordination of women and strategies of power, the Christian faith in an emotional culture and the year 2000: reality and hope); we also regret the absence of other issues, like the debate on the transformation of the attitude of the church towards Judaism. However, the aim of the articles is in no way to discuss every aspect of these questions. Rather, we want to show their place in the wider theological whole; to demonstrate how they are symptomatic and what alternatives they open up, or, possibly, what decisions they await.

In the first part Giuseppe Ruggieri asks whether the Council did not introduce a quite new method of facing the questions put to the church by history; the central part of the issue then surveys some of the major questions in dispute at present, grouping them under the headings usual in *Concilium*.

The fundamental debate on the church's use of the scriptures (Freyne) is followed by several approaches along the main lines of Christian faith: the humanity of Christ (Moingt), the spiritual identity of the Christian (Moltmann), God from the perspective of the victims of history (Theobald and Mieth) and a new way of encountering our neighbours of other religions (Wilfred).

And since believing is first perceived in the body in which it takes place – the many life-styles of Christians and their contemporaries – here too the debates on ethical questions, though too often selective, have to be introduced (Ammicht-Quinn and Mieth). In an adjacent area there is a discussion of the hermeneutical problem of the regulation of faith and the fear of a creative reception, even though such a reception was the main issue in Vatican II (Theobald).

The following articles move in a strictly ecclesial area: the demand for a permanent reform which will benefit from the contribution of ideological criticism (Schüssler Fiorenza), the conciliarity of the church (Berlis), etc. Because of its importance, the question of the future of the local churches (Beozzo) has been dealt with in a long documentation at the end of this issue, although logically it has its place in this section. This ecclesiological group ends with a fundamental reflection on the inter-confessional and intercultural mutations in the theology of mission (Collet).

The last series of articles deals with some problems of culture and the practical way in which they are dealt with by the church: the diagnosis of the present moment (Junker-Kenny), cultural amnesia (Duqoc), fundamentalism and the phenomenon of the sects, even within the church (Tomka), and finally the difficult relationship between aesthetics and religion (Kuschel).

Of course we are not suggesting to readers the agenda for a future Vatican III. Our selection of 'unanswered questions' is too narrow for that, and perhaps is an arbitrary one. Besides, it is not certain that the time for such an ecumenical assembly has come. Rather, we need to enter collectively into a period of experimentation in which the church accepts becoming more like a laboratory in which many experiments are being carried on, doubtless with unforeseen results. Pastors have found it difficult to accept this kind of conciliarity of experiences, which calls for a new way of understanding Catholicity, a way which is less legalistic and more sensitive to the difference between cultural contexts, and more in keeping with the gospel in the way in which it preserves unity in faith.

The two editors set out to show this way in the final part, reflecting on the turning point which is indicated by the questions touched on in the issue; on the form of communication which dealing with them requires; and on the nearness of the holy God, always more human, whose concerns they bear.

It will be noted that most of the contributors to this issue come from the committee of the directors of *Concilium*. Faithful to its conciliar tradition, in this way *Concilium* seeks to express once more a questioning which is both demanding and confident.

Christoph Theobald and Dietmar Mieth

Part I

Towards a Hermeneutic of Vatican II

Giuseppe Ruggieri

Like any living organism, from the beginning the church too has had to react to the internal and external demands made on it, in other words to redefine itself in the human context of its own time. In the primitive community, the questions included: What conditions are to be imposed on the pagans who embrace the gospel? What is the sense of sexual relations and is it permissible to marry, given that the coming of the Lord is imminent? What is the relationship between the Mosaic Law, Greek wisdom and the gospel? The subsequent history of the church increased the number of questions. It did so for two reasons: because new questions arose and because the previous answers proved inadequate. New questions were: what to do with the Hebrew scriptures, what to do with those who had committed serious sins after baptism, what to do with those who had denied the faith in a time of persecution, what to do with those who had bought their ordination (simony), what to do in the face of the abuses of power in the church, what to do in the face of the corruption of Christian life at the top and at the grass roots? But also, later: What are the rights of the Indios? What does it mean to take the gospel to a society like that of China? What is the relationship between modern reason and the Christian revelation?

Today there are so many questions, some of which will be raised in this issue of *Concilium*: from the use of scripture (as always!), the Petrine ministry, 'holistic' religion in post-modern culture, the theologies of liberation, to the future of Christian ecumenism, and so on.

The question which I want to discuss here is whether and how the Second Vatican Council can help to answer the questions which are arising in the Christian churches today. More precisely, I want to ask whether a method was not inaugurated at the last Council for facing the great questions which history puts to the church that was in some way new. The question is all the more urgent, in that perplexity is rife. Doesn't this Council now belong to the past? It may have ended one era of the church, but what can it offer today? And, even accepting that the decisions of the Second Vatican Council are still of some use today, how are we to distinguish between these decisions, inasmuch as everyone, even those who think in an opposite way, seems to appeal to the Council?

Reference back to the Council is in fact in many respects in danger of becoming almost a commonplace. But if one looks at the diversity of interpretations, this apparent commonplace now increasingly recalls a brutal image that an eleventh-century author applied to those who, during the Gregorian controversy, used the authority of scripture at will, taking the same text from one part or another: 'They have not understood scripture correctly. In fact they have milked its breast violently, and instead of milk have drunk blood.'[1] Is it possible not to do violence to Vatican II? Is it possible to recognize in it, while respecting historical truth, indications which are useful for answering the questions that we raise after two thousand years of Christian history?

What was the Council?

The struggle over the significance of the Council exploded with particular virulence immediately after it ended. In fact the extreme minority which already during the work of the Council was opposed to taking up the great tradition of the church (a tradition that could not be confined to the pronouncements of the magisterium over the last two centuries and that was far more varied within the church than the neoscholastic garb imposed from the second half of the nineteenth century onwards claimed) and to *aggiornamento* in the sense desired by Pope John XXIII, made their own refutation of the Council, arguing that it was in error.[2] In fact the Council was said to be a betrayal of the post-Tridentine Catholic tradition both in its liturgical and its doctrinal innovations (scripture and tradition, collegiality, etc.) and in its openness to secularized culture as expressed above all in the constitution *Gaudium et spes*.

The youth 'revolution' of 1968 in America and Western Europe exacerbated the conflict between the interpretations. It was in fact argued, in that climate which saw the beginning of 'dreams of power', that the Council had definitively closed an era, representing so to speak a 'break' in the tradition of the church. The slogan 'the end of the Counter-Reformation',[3] while intrinsically justified, came to be loaded with exaggerated meaning, to the point of making Vatican II an event which itself belonged to the Eurocentric past.

Between Scylla and Charybdis, between integralism and the challenge from the left, others called for a return to the 'documents' as an antidote to what was claimed to be being done on the basis of the 'spirit' of the Council.[4] Yet others, seeking to bring the Council within the traditional confines of theological hermeneutics, demanded that the Council should be interpreted within the continuity of Catholic reality.[5]

This simple listing of some of the interpretations of Vatican II in the Catholic Church – and it is also worth recalling at least the interpretation offered by the Synod of Bishops in 1985[6] – already shows the need for a historical reconstruction of the event of the Council. Moreover this has already begun.[7] Here I shall develop only three points which are of great methodological interest. The first, which seeks to bring together some elements of the 'spirit' of the conciliar event, already takes up some indications of historical research into the last Council; the second, which tries to put the conciliar shift in the context of the church's tradition, goes back to a well-known interpretative hypothesis put forward by Karl Rahner; the third, finally, seeks to make some hermeneutical comments on 'signs of the times', a central methodological point of Vatican II.

From reform to *aggiornamento*[8]

Vatican II represents a new development in respect of the past, but not in the sense that it ignores tradition. However, it can be quietly stated that it was much more respectful of the church than was, for example, Vatican I.[9] In Vatican II, as compared to the 1870 Council, there was a concern to go back to the ancient sources of the life of the church, without being limited to developments in the past 150 years; this was the precise opposite of a mentality which was afraid of the vastness of the global tradition of the church and preferred not to change the tranquil and limited equilibrium of the immediate past.

The main novelty of Vatican II was rather its consideration of history as related to the gospel and the Christian truth. Whereas for the most part in the past there had been an awareness that history as experienced by human beings was ultimately of no importance for the understanding of the gospel (I use the term 'awareness', although 'in reality' it was never such a thing), the major question of the Second Vatican Council was precisely this, even if the words used (pastoral nature, *aggiornamento*, signs of the time) were not immediately understood clearly by all. This can be illustrated by a large number of examples. It is enough to quote one of them here, the discussion that took place during the first phase of the Council on the first doctrinal document, which was to become the constitution *Dei Verbum* but at that time was called *De fontibus revelationis*. At that time the discussion was on the 'pastoral character' of the doctrine of revelation rather than on details of its content. On the one hand there were those who repeated the old distinction between a doctrine which was to be clear and concise, respecting, as Cardinal Ottaviani said, 'the praxis of the centuries'. On the other hand there were those who, drawing strength from the position of John XXIII which had emerged with the utmost clarity and authority in the opening allocution *Gaudet mater ecclesia*, thought that this doctrine was to be formulated taking into account the needs of contemporary men and women.[10]

For John XXIII, the interpretation of the gospel was inseparable from the reference to history. For him in fact, every time, in order to enter more deeply into a doctrine, it was necessary to reformulate the substance of the gospel according to the needs of the times. This reformulation was a requirement of 'continuity' and not a break:

> In fact we have to understand that innovation is part of the very nature of Christian doctrine, which respects the internal balance of its substance, formulated in time, by remaining identical to itself. The formulation of the outward appearance does not then appear as something ephemeral, but each time as a new historical imperative which a magisterium with a predominantly pastoral character needs to take into account. Thus pastoral connotations come to find a place within the doctrinal dimension of Christianity, as an intrinsic requirement for doctrine to present its substance in time: *the pastoral dimension as a historical hermeneutic of Christian truth*.[11]

The old idea of the reform of the church, when confronted with the pastoral *aggiornamento* of Pope Roncalli, had a different balance with history. It in fact called for the restoration of the authentic form of the church, to remedy the deformations of its primitive form which had taken place and the abuses which had come about in both head and members. This idea was not negated by that of *aggiornamento*, but was now steeped in a more vital context which John XXIII expressed with the ideas of the renewal of the church, the garden to be looked after and not the museum to be conserved, etc.

So now it was a matter of rediscovering in depth the significance, as a historical *locus*, of history lived and interpreted by human beings. It should be noted that the concern was to speak of history as actually *lived* and not simply of history *told*, as it had been conceived by the traditional treatise dealing with *loci theologici*.[12] That approach saw history as a totality of sources and documents from which arguments could be drawn in support of the truth affirmed in the church. Only if it recalls history as lived out and interpreted by men and women does the category of the signs of the times become central. But this implies another task which still has to be faced, namely the 'overcoming of the hegemony of "theology", understood as the isolation of the doctrinal dimension of faith and its abstract conceptualization, and that of "legalism,", which rigidifies the dynamism of Christian experience in legal formulae'.[13]

The Council as a beginning

Karl Rahner, in a perceptive reading of the historical significance of the last council for theology,[14] argued that to some degree the break marked by the Council could be compared only to that at the beginning of the primitive church when the disciples, in the power of the spirit of the risen Christ, took initiatives which did not represent the simple continuation of the teaching of Jesus: 'We today are living for the first time in the period of such a break, which took place only in the transition from Jewish Christianity to pagan Christianity.' As a consequence of this interpretation, the significance of Vatican II lies in the fact that 'in it, even if only in an initial and unclear way, the church has proclaimed the transition from the Western church to a universal church in a sense which hitherto took place for the first and only time when the church of the Jews became a church of the pagans'. This interpretative hypothesis opens up a series of questions, the first of which is: 'whether and to what degree the church still, in the post-apostolic period, has the power and the creative energy which it had and claimed to have at the time of its first beginnings, to take basic irreversible, or apparently irreversible decisions which for the first time would constitute it in its concrete nature, beyond that which has attributed to it with immediate directness by the Risen Jesus'. And another basic question remains open: whether and to what the degree the church, now confronted with a new break, can perceive possibilities which it never used before because this would have been illegitimate.

As is evident from the last comment, once Rahner's interpretative hypothesis is accepted, the consequence should not be a nullification of church tradition. Just as the disciples, confronted with the 'absent third party', i.e. confronted with a new cultural subject other than the traditional Jewish subject and the new Christian subject that they themselves were,[15] had to rethink the Old Testament and Jewish culture creatively on the basis of their faith in Jesus Christ, so the churches have to rethink their faith today. Here we find ourselves facing a new beginning. In an unprecedented form, a pluralism of culture and peoples is emerging which, in the historical awareness that we now have of this pluralism and its dignity, is not comparable with that of past eras. But the 'beginning' is not an absolute beginning. That would be unthinkable for Christians. No one can build on a foundation other than that 'which has been laid'. Rather, it is a matter of a creative interpretation which rediscovers possibilities in the tradition of which it has never previously made use, because past history did not draw on them or even thought that they were ruled out.

Moreover this was the true significance of the great debate on tradition which took place in Vatican II. It was a debate which did not have a satisfactory outcome. It still remained too much a prisoner of the post-Tridentine climate, stretched as it was between the recovery of the 'living' tradition on the one hand and the challenge to this vitalistic conception of the tradition by the ultra-conservatives, but also by those who did not want to abolish the normative function of scripture for the successive developments of the church's tradition.[16] An Eastern bishop, N. Edelby, was able to note in his contribution to the Council how this discussion remained wholly within the Latin tradition, a prisoner of the legalistic interpretative opposition between scripture and tradition. For his part, he proposed a conception of the 'tradition as an epiclesis of the history of salvation, that is, a theophany of the Holy Spirit, without which the history of the world cannot be understood and holy scripture remains a dead letter'.[17]

The signs of the times

The problem is to rediscover the precise link between history and the Spirit of Christ, in such a way that the new questions of history make it possible to understand the gospel again in time. So that makes a theology of the signs of the time necessary. However, other than inflating the expression so that it has come to be used more to indicate the characteristic features of our period of history, post-conciliar theology has not learned to deepen the theological hermeneutical significance of this category.[18]

Although it was already present earlier, above all in the theology and preaching of nineteenth-century Protestantism, but also in Catholic theology (Chenu!) and the Catholic writing of the first half of our century, it made its 'official' entry into Catholic theology on 25 December 1961, through the Bull heralding Vatican II, *Humanae salutis*. Pope Roncalli wrote that 'making our own the exhortation of Jesus to know how to discern the "signs of the times" (Matt. 16.4), we seem to perceive in the midst of so much darkness a number of indications which give hope for the future of the church and humankind'. The Council was in turn to take up the expression four times in its final documents,[19] though the concept as such appears more often. The expression has positive and hopeful connotations, but its main significance cannot be reduced to this.

The fact that a pope could claim to read positive signs 'which give hope for the future of the church and humankind' in the concrete history of his own time might today appear trivial or unimportant. However, with John XXIII the expression had been carefully thought out and was meant to correct a vision which was to some degree dominant in the tradition of the Catholic Church, from the nineteenth-century Restoration right through the first half of the twentieth century (that of the 'prophets of doom'). From the French Revolution onwards, in fact the Catholic magisterium had become hardened in a negative evaluation of modern history.[20] As an 'ideal' basis for this evaluation, which in turn had its roots in eighteenth-century apologetics, one could cite the encyclical *Mirari vos* of Gregory XVI (15 August 1832), who read contemporary history under the sign of a 'conspiracy of wicked men'. This perspective did not allow any indulgence and benevolence on the part of the church, but rather forced it to suppress the various errors 'with the stick'. This sweeping negative judgment on history and Western society, above all on the democratic societies, was not only taken up in the magisterium of Pius XI (one need only cite the *Syllabus*) but so to speak solemnly codified in the preface which opens the Dogmatic Constitution of Vatican I on the Catholic Faith: modern history, after the Council of Trent, is described as a progressive corruption of human beings, provoked by the Protestant negation of the principle of authority.

It is in this context that we need to see the significance of the key words of the magisterium of John XXIII. The category of 'signs of the times' is thus consistent with that of pastoral nature and *aggiornamento* and represents his own conception of Christian doctrine and the magisterium. Thus the signs of the times make it possible to rediscover the youth of the gospel, drawing from it, through the Spirit, possibilities which earlier interpretations had not grasped. If we look carefully, this is the significance of the conception of the tradition as the 'epiclesis' of the Spirit in history (Edelby), which emphasizes that now it is the history actually lived out by human beings that must be invested with the energy of the spirit of Christ. The theological historical significance of the category of signs of the times lies here. History, not just of the past but above all of the present, with the vicissitudes experienced by men and women in our time, is a *locus theologicus*.[21] As I have already indicated, this statement does not express the traditional view which considered above all narrated history, the documents of the past from which evidence of true Catholicism could be drawn, as a theological *locus*.

Neither simple documented history, nor even simple history as experienced, can produce the distinctive signs as a place for a renewed presence of the Spirit of Christ. Moreover history is always mediated by a culture, by a collective memory and, in the societies in which an organized transmission of knowledge flourishes, by reflections stemming from the critical knowledge of history itself. Human history exists above all where there is conscious awareness, with a critical basis, of the significance of human affairs and events experienced in the present, not only as the fruit of the possibilities laid down by people in the past but also as a destruction of those possibilities and therefore as a negation. There are also ruins in history, things which disappear for ever, like the blood of Abel, and have no future or descendants. A vision of history which maintains the memory of its sufferings and therefore struggles for a reconciled future is precisely what is mediated by messianic expectations.[22]

But this indicates the possibility of an integration of history and its distinctive signs, less 'extrinsic' than Cano himself thought, into theological knowledge. Vatican II, in the constitution *Gaudium et Spes* no.44, explicitly recognizes this non-extrinsic character of human history when it affirms that the church 'does not ignore what it has received from history and from the development of the human race' (*Gaudium et Spes* 44). So it speaks of a *commercium augendum*, a growing exchange between history and church, above all in evangelization.[23]

This affirmation obviously presupposes that the Christian economy of salvation is a historical economy, and is therefore in the making. The cognitive role of the sign of the times must not remain the prisoner of an 'objectivistic' conception of the Christian revelation, failing to see that this revelation not only has its 'founding' movement but is also always in action.[24] The signs of the times are not 'external' to the economy of salvation, but go to constitute it, together with the epiclesis of the Spirit of Christ, crucified and risen.

Moreover, in the only passage in the New Testament in which it appears, Matt. 16.3, the expression 'signs of the times' denotes the signs of the messianic time, that is the words and actions of Jesus of Nazareth. Christ realizes the messianic times foreseen by the prophets, which his interlocutors are unable to see. The parallel passage, Luke 12.53, does not have the expression 'signs of the times', but *kairos*, the specific time in which the grace of God is offered to men and women. In Luke, as in Matthew, the significance of the expression is therefore christological and eschatological at the same time. In some way the one sign of the times is Christ himself. From him and from the presence of Christ in the church, through his spirit but also in all creation, it is possible to document how in the New Testament this *kairos*, this opportune moment of grace, runs through all history until the last coming and the final reconciliation of all things.

The basic hermeneutical question thus has to be formulated like this: why does the kingdom of God come in the history of Jesus of Nazareth? Why must we recognize in it the sign of the times, the *kairos*? It should be noted that this is not only a positive history, that of miracles, but also a negative history, just as its decisive moment is Jesus' death on the cross, the abandonment by God (Auschwitz and Hiroshima!), the descent into hell, at least if we understand this as the prolongation of the abandonment of God on the cross (thus Hans Urs von Balthasar).

The reply that can be given from the global perspective of the New Testament is that in Christ God has reached every human being and every thing, reconciling them with himself, 'exchanging them' with Christ, inasmuch as Christ is this global reconciliation/exchange. In him the kingdom comes, so he is the long-awaited sign of the times, because in him God reaches and welcomes every man and woman: in the first place the one who was lost, the sinner.[25] Nothing illustrates this better than the text of II Cor. 5.17–21. Here the novelty of the Christian event is grounded in an 'exchange'. In fact the one who did not know sin has been made sin, because 'in him' we have become the justice of God. In this exchange that is the ultimate essence of the christological event, in which every sinner is reached by God, we have therefore been reconciled with God. In Christ every human being has been welcomed in God. With another Pauline expression, we can say that in Christ there is God's definitive 'Yes' to human beings. The messianic kingdom takes place in the gift of Christ to human beings, and because of that he is 'the sign of the times'; in him the old things are past and new things are born.

What needs to be noted for a hermeneutic of the signs of the times is the conviction of the believer that in Christ *all* history, including that of death and sin, has been reached and redeemed. Not only the healing of the sick and bread for the starving multitudes but also death and annihilation are, in the christological 'exchange', signals of the advent of God in history. Even the absence of God ('My God, my God, why have you forsaken me?') which constitutes the experience of death is recognized a 'death for': his body has been given for us, he died for our sins, etc.

Another way of approaching the heart of the problem is also opened up by the historiographical discussion, above all in the French-speaking world, of the relationship between *longue durée* and *événement*. Within the so-called *'Annales'* school there was a marked tendency to emphasize long-term factors, the constants (climatic, economic, mental etc.) of human life, while events, 'the facts that people talk about', were considered more as signs indicative of the long-term reality and its supporting structures. Against this tendency, however, more recently there has been a reassertion of the role of the event, of a fact or a series of facts which determine the transition from one structure to another, and which therefore introduce innovations into history.[26] By extrapolating the terms of this discussion we can say that, since an event introduces a new element into history, it can modify those structures of human relationships which constituted the former equilibrium. There is no denying the fact, for example, that the Lutheran Reformation, along with all the factors which constituted it – from Luther's preaching to the pamphlets which spread his thought and created the first real large movement of opinion in modern history, from the involvement of some social classes in it to the emergence of a 'new' ecclesial subject like the laity – was an event capable of changing the religious life of the European peoples in the long term. Again it is probable, to take a contemporary example, that Vatican II has been an event capable of modifying substantially the mentality and behaviour of all Christians, and not just the Catholics of our time.[27] In the light of these reflections we can attempt a last definition of the signs of the time. A fact is capable of becoming a sign of the times when, *thanks to a collective awareness*, it is capable of modifying *in a messianic direction* the equilibrium of human relations in a particular era. Why this happens is determined by the collective awareness. The possible submarine eruption which could change the climatic balance of the planet is not yet a sign of the time. But the collective awareness of the destruction of nature brought about by the destructive culture of *homo faber*, a collective awareness which is contributing towards bringing about a new sense of responsibility towards future generations, is a sign of the times. This awareness, and not the destruction of nature as such, presages a future with fewer deaths, with a less violent and more sober life-style, so that we can legitimately see it as sign of the creation which looks to liberation.

It is enough to give one more example to end with. The poverty in which indeterminate numbers of people live is not yet a sign of the time. It is not even a sign of the time when it provokes a movement of solidarity. The history of the church is full of testimonies of good deeds towards the poor but, perhaps with the exception of the first days of the Franciscans, this has not led to an effective rethinking of the gospel. Only when some people begin to put poverty in a messianic light and discover a new equilibrium in the gospel and the church, so that the mystery of poverty – among the poor and in Christ who made himself poor – becomes the axis of history, the gospel becomes the gospel of the poor and the church becomes the church of the poor, do people begin to recognize a sign of the times.[28]

Epilogue against proof-texts

When the Council stops being a series of texts with which one's own theological and practical choices are proved; when, that is, we get past the phase of using the Council as a collection of proof-texts, and rediscover its spirit through a rigorous awareness of the whole event of the Council, we shall be able to get a little milk. Milk, in the image of the mediaeval author whom I quoted at the beginning, is opposed to the blood of violence, and suggests rather the gentleness and the humility of the one who does not resist the spirit that prays within us and opens history to the gospel of the Crucified.

Translated by John Bowden

Notes

1. *Libelli de Lite* 1, MGH, Scriptores 9, Hanover 1891, 256.
2. Cf. D. Menozzi, 'L'anticoncilio (1966–1984)', in *Il Vaticano II e la Chiesa*, Brescia 1985, 433–64.
3. The first to have formulated this seems to have been, at the end of the first conciliar period, P. Rouquette, who wrote in the January issue of *Etudes* (p. 104), 'the era of the Counter-Reformation is over'.
4. Thus Cardinal Ratzinger, in *Rapporto sulla fede. Vittorio Messori a colloquio con Joseph Ratzinger*, Cinisello Balsamo 1985, 32–3. But this cannot mean that there is not an authentic spirit of the conciliar event in the light of which its decisions are to be interpreted. In that case the problem remains, and becomes that of how this spirit of the Council is to be understood.
5. W. Kasper, *Theology and Church*, London 1989, 166–76. The demand is a fair one, provided that it does not deprive the event of its originality: cf. the observations by P. Hünermann, 'Il concilio Vaticano II come evento', in M. T. Fattori and A. Melloni, *L'evento e le decisioni. Studi sulle dinamiche del concilio Vaticano II*, Bologna 1997, esp. 67–70.
6. Cf. *Concilium* 1986/6.
7. Above all by the group of historians who, with G. Alberigo, have in recent years already started a *History of the Second Vatican Council*.
8. Historical and theological statements are made in this section which are documented in G. Alberigo, 'L'amore alla chiesa: della riforma all'aggiornamento', in A. and G. Alberigo, *'Con tutte le tue forze.' I nodi della fede cristiana oggi, Omaggio a Giuseppe Dossetti*, Genoa 1993, 159–94; id., 'Réforme ou "aggironamento" de l'église?', in *Communion et réunion. Mélanges Jean-Marie Roger Tillard*, Leuven 1995, 323–32; G. Ruggieri, 'Appunti per una teologia in Papa Roncalli', in G. Alberigo, *Papa Giovanni*, Bari 1987, 245–71; id., 'La discussione sullo schema Constitutionis dogmaticae de fontibus revelationis durante la I sessione del concilio Vaticano I', in E.

Fouilloux, *Vatican II commence . . . Approches Francophones*, Leuven 1993, 291–328; id., 'La lotta per la pastoralità della dottrina: le recenzione della *Gaudet Mater Ecclesia* net primo periodo del concilio Vaticano II', in W. Weiss (ed.), *Zeugnis und Dialog. Die katholische Kirche in der neuzeitlichen Welt und das II. Vatikanische Konzil. Klaus Wittstadt zum 60. Geburtstag*, Würzburg 1996, 118–37.

9. Cf. G. Alberigo, 'Die Rezeption der grossen christlichen Überlieferung durch das zweite Vatikanische Konzil', in W. Löser, K. Lehmann and M. Lutz-Bachmann, *Dogmengeschichte und katholische Theologie,* Würzburg 1985, 303–20; A. Dulles, 'Das III. Vatikanum and die Wierdergewinnung der Tradition', in E. Klinger and K. Wittstadt, *Glaube im Prozess. Christsein nach dem II. Vatikanum. Für Karl Rahner,* Freiburg, Basel and Vienna 1985, 546–62.

10. Cf. G. Ruggieri, 'Il primo conflitto dottrinale', in G. Alberigo, *Storia del concilio Vaticano II,* Vol. 2, Bologna 1996, 259–93.

11. Ruggieri, 'Appunti per una teologia in Papa Roncalli' (n.8), 256.

12. Here I am referring to the scholastic manuals and not to the thought of Melchior Cano as such. For him see the recent research by B. Körner, *Melchior Cano. De locis theologicis. Ein Beitrag zur theologischen Erkenntnislehre*, Graz 1994.

13. Alberigo, 'L'amore alla chiesa' (n.8), 193.

14. Cf. K. Rahner, 'Basic Theological Interpretation of the Second Vatican Council', in *Theological Investigations* 20, London 1981, 77–89. The developments of Rahner's interpretation in J. B. Metz, 'Im Aufbruch einer kulturell polyzentrischen Weltkirche', in F.-X. Kaufmann and J. B. Metz, *Zukunftsfähigkeit. Suchbewegungen in Christentum*, Freiburg, Basel and Vienna, 92–123; id., 'Das Konzil "der Anfang eines Anfangs"', in K. Richter (ed.), *Das Konzil war erst der Anfang, Die Bedeutung des II. Vatikanums für Theologie und Kirche*, Mainz 1991, 11–24, are also important. However, we should recall another important historical and theological periodization of the Council, according to which in the history of the church there is not only the break with the primitive church but also the break with the Constantinian era, so that Vatican II would amount to a third break. This is the reading which M-D. Chenu already gave during the preparatory period: 'La fin de l'ère constantinienne', in *Un concile pour notre temps. Journées d'études des "Informations catholiques internationales"*, Paris 1961, 59–87.

15. The 'absent third party' here is a reference to the reflections by M. de Certeau; ef. J. Moingt, 'Une théologie de l'exil', in C. Geffré (ed.), *Michel de Certeau ou la différence chrétienne. Actes du colloque 'Michel de Certeau et le christianisme'*, Paris 1991, 129–56.

16. Cf. the comment by J. Ratzinger, in 'Das Zweite Vatikanische Konzil', *LThK* 2, 518ff.; A. Franzini, *Tradizione e scrittura. Il contributo del concilio Vaticano II*, Rome 1977; for the post-conciliar discussion see recently A. Buckenmaier, '*Schrift und Tradition' seit dem Vatikanum II. Vorgeschichte und Rezeption*, Paderborn 1996; for a general reflection cf. D. Wiederkehr (ed.), *Wie geschieht Tradition. Überlieferung im Lebenzprozess der Kirche*, Freiburg, Basel and Vienna 1991.

17. *Acta Synodalia Sacrosancti Concilii Oecumenici Vaticani II*, III/3, 307.

18. After the first series of studies, immediately following the Council, there was a new surge of interest. Moreover, even in recent studies there is a sociological reduction of the category.

19. *Gaudium et spes* 4; *Presbyterorum ordinis* 9; *Apostolicam actuositatem* 14; *Unitatis redintegratio* 4.

20. Cf. G. Alberigo, 'Dal bastone alla misericordia. Il magistero nel cattolicesimo contemporaneo (1830–1980)', in *Cristianesimo nella storia* 2, 1981, 487–521.

21. I have tried to develop some reflections on this in 'La storia come luogo teologico', *Laurentianum* 35, 1994, 319–37. I take up some of them here.

22. Here the thought of W. Benjamin, above all as expressed in 'Theologisch-politisches Fragment', *Gesammelte Scriften* II. 1, 203–4; II, 3, 946–9 and 'Über den Begriff der Geschichte', ibid. I, 2, 691–704; I, 3, 1223–66, is still topical here; these thoughts have been taken up theologically in a particularly incisive way by J. B. Metz, 'Hoffnung als Naherwartung oder der Kampf um die verlorene Zeit. Unzeitgemässe Thesen zur Apokalyptik', in *Glaube in Geschichte und Gesellschaft*, Maniz 1997, 49–58.

23. For a global examination of the consideration of history in Vatican II see still G. Alberigo, 'Cristianesimo e storia nel Vaticano II', in *Cristianesimo nella storia* V/3, 1984, 577–92. But it is significant that this author comments how 'the most decisive indications seem to be those contained in the constitutions on the liturgy, on the church and on the word of God, in that they show *in action* (my emphasis) the relevance of the historical condition of Christianity' (591). We need to pay attention not only to the explicit consideration of history present in the Council, but also to the presence of a historical awareness which is implicit and operative in other assertions of the Council.

24. Cf. Yves Congar, *La tradizione e le tradizioni, I. Saggio storico*, Rome 1961, 220–47.

25. For a christology of 'exchange' on the biblical level see M. D. Hooker, 'Interchange in Christ', *Journal of Theological Studies* NS 22, 1971, 349–61; 'Philippians 2.6–11', in *Jesus and Paulus. Festschrift W. G. Kümmel*, Göttingen 1975, 151–64; the Pauline texts on 'exchange' have been analysed by S. E. Porter, in *Ancient Greek Writing with reference to the Pauline Writings*, Cordoba 1994; on the level of theological reflection cf. E. Przywara, 'Commercium', in *Logos*, Düsseldorf 1964, 119–65.

26. As extreme representatives of the discussion can be cited on the one hand Fernand Braduel, for whom history was an applied social science which analyses the perennial structures and models which arise above the somewhat dusky surface of human events and, at the extreme opposite, Pierre Nora, who prefers the event, conceived of as the effect that the knowledge of a more or less important fact has on social groups to the point of inducing them to change attitude. It is clear that according to this second extreme view the event is possibly only in that it is known and arises only in the contemporary period, when by means of social communication it becomes possible to draw attention to an event; cf. *L'événement. Actes du Colloque organisé à Aix-en-Provence par le Centre Meridionale d'Histoire Sociale, le 16, 17, et 18 September 1983*, Aix-en-Provence 1986; P. Burke, *The French Historical Revolution. The 'Annales' School 1929–1989*, Stanford 1990.

27. Cf. E. Fouilloux, 'La Categoria di evento nella storiografia francese recente', in *L'evento e le decisioni. Studi sulle dinamiche del concilio Vaticano II*, ed. M. T. Fattoria and A. Melloni, Bologna 1997, 51–62; J. A. Komonchak, 'Riflessioni storiografiche sul Vaticano II come evento', ibid., 417–39.

28. Cf. the conciliar discourse of Cardinal Lerari given on 6 December 1962, now in G. Lercaro, *Per la forza dello Spirito*, Bologna 1984, 113–22, and his other interventions on poverty, ibid., 123–70.

Part II · A Selection of Questions

The Bible and Theology.
An Unresolved Tension

Seán Freyne

One of my abiding memories of my first visit to Rome in the early 1960s to begin biblical studies there is the furore that arose, even prior to the first session of the Council, concerning the draft proposal on divine revelation, prepared by the Holy Office. The Bea and Ottaviani factions, as the opposing positions came to be labelled, represented two very different trends – the former calling for the implementation of the historical-critical method in the study of the Bible, following the influential encyclical of Pope Pius XII, *Divino Afflante Spiritu* (1943), and the latter seeking to restore the pre-critical, 'spiritual' approach which had persisted in Catholic circles since the patristic age. The matter was finally resolved by the intervention of Pope John XXIII and the production of a new draft which eventually was approved as the constitution *Dei Verbum* in 1965.

Another memory from those days is the image of an open copy of the Bible in the assembly hall of the Council, a symbolic reminder to the Fathers that the purpose of this Council was pastoral rather than doctrinal. The task was to open the Scriptures to the people of God, so that their Spirit would henceforth inform the whole life of the church. Such a decision was truly momentous in view of the limited role that the Bible had played in Catholic circles ever since the sixteenth-century Reformation. The Bible was to be 'the soul of Theology' (*Dei Verbum* 24), no longer to be treated as a mere collection of proof-texts.

Thirty-five years later it must be said that this ideal is far from realized, despite the production of the Lectionary for use in the liturgy, which has offered a wide range of readings from both Testaments for the spiritual nourishment of the people of God. The failure of most homilists to

actualize these readings in terms of contemporary life and culture
suggests that something is amiss with the teaching of the Bible in national
seminaries, not just in Ireland, my homeland, but in several other
European countries of my experience. Could it be that despite all the
fine sentiments of *Dei Verbum*, the Counter-Reformation preference for
sacrament over word is still alive and well in Roman Catholicism? Karl
Rahner's claim, namely, that at the Reformation they (Protestants) took
the Book and we (Catholics) took the Sacrament, to the mutual
impoverishment of both, would appear to be still operative, at least in
some circles.

It is in the area of Catholic theology that the failure to implement the
Council's vision has had the most far-reaching effects on the life of the
church. Especially when the use of scripture in theology is examined in
some recent official documents, it would seem that the pre-critical stance
which *Divino Afflante Spiritu* had sought to correct twenty years before
the Council is once more in danger of becoming the dominant trend.

To substantiate that claim one has only to examine the way in which
Scripture is appropriated in *The Catechism of the Catholic Church* (1994).
As several commentators have noted, this work, while basing itself on
conciliar documents, is both selective and restrictive in many respects
with regards to its primary source.[1] For example, in dealing with the role
of the Bible in the life of the church, it contents itself with a few general
exhortations, even though the topic greatly exercised the Fathers of the
Council (*Dei Verbum*, 21–26; cf. *Catechism*, 131–3). On the other hand
the *Catechism* lays a special emphasis on the role of the magisterium (the
Pope and Bishops) in the interpretation of scripture (*Catechism*, 85–6),
omitting many others – exegetes, catechists, etc. – who are involved in the
ministry of the word as the Council had insisted (*Dei Verbum*, 23–25).

This 'reclaiming' of the interpretation of the Bible for the official
magisterium is disturbing, not only because it ignores the gift of the
Spirit to the whole church, but because it is accompanied by a naive
literalism throughout the work. In dealing with the origins of the human
race, for example, the symbolic/figurative nature of the Genesis stories is
recognized, but it is claimed at the same time that the account of the Fall
in Genesis 3 'affirms a primeval event, a deed that took place *at the
beginning of the history of man*' (*Catechism*, 390, italics in the original). It is
as though more than a century of debate about the mythological nature of
these chapters had never taken place.[2]

Another example of current theological interest is the sacrament of
order in its three grades of deacon, priest and bishop (*Catechism*, 1578–
80).[3] Not surprisingly, women are deemed to be excluded from all three,
and once again scripture is used in a very uncritical and ahistorical

manner to sustain this position, following the lines of the more extended treatment by Pope John Paul II in his apostolic letter *Mulieris Dignitatem* (26–27). Jesus only chose men (*viri*) to form the college of the twelve apostles, and this college remains an ever-present reality through the college of bishops and priests (deacons are not mentioned at this point). Women are thereby excluded, 'since the Church recognizes herself to be bound by the choice made by the Lord himself' (1577). This is indeed a curious line of argumentation, with a definite *ad hoc* ring to it. The Twelve represent a once-only group in the ministry of Jesus and members were not in fact replaced, after they died, with the exception of the traitor, Judas. It clearly had a symbolic role with regard to the restoration of Israel within the ministry of Jesus, but as the focus and scope of the mission changed it lost that significance and the group disappeared from view. Indeed the various lists of names of the members are not wholly consistent.[4] It is only relatively late that Luke combined the Pauline title 'apostle' with the Twelve, even though the term had a wider application, including also a woman (Junia, in Rom. 16.7). To attempt to reduce the origin and status of the whole of Christian ministry to the group of the Twelve is, therefore, quite unhistorical, and pays no attention to the developments and fluidity of roles for women and men that were part of the early Christian church, as can be seen in almost every document of the New Testament.

These examples will have to suffice to explain the unease of many commentators with regard to the *Catechism's* use of Scripture. It smacks of a return to the pre-critical proof-texting use of the Bible in order to support positions that have been arrived at by very different criteria. In such a climate it is difficult to see how the Bible can really function as the Word of God, whose cutting edge can penetrate to the heart of all human constructions, even those of the magisterium itself.

This approach is all the more surprising in the light of the 1994 Instruction. *The Interpretation of the Bible in the Church*.[5] True, this document emanated from the Pontifical Biblical Commission, and in the preface Cardinal Ratzinger acknowledges that in its 'new form' the Commission 'is not an organ of the teaching office', but a group of scholars who, because of their responsible scholarship as believing exegetes, have the confidence of the teaching office. Clearly, the Cardinal sees no conflict between ecclesial loyalty and scholarly scientific study of the Bible. In his address endorsing the document on the occasion of the centenary of Leo XIII's encyclical on biblical interpretation, *Providentissimus Deus*, Pope John Paul II recognizes the changing intellectual climate in which over the previous hundred years the Catholic Church had approached the scientific study of the Bible. In particular he draws attention to the fact that *Divino Afflante Spiritu* of Pope Pius XII had highlighted the need for the use of the historical-critical method, against its detractors within the church who wanted the 'spiritual' or 'mystical' approach, with its ahistorical presuppositions, restored.

Against this background, the Instruction itself presents a thoroughly up-to-date account of contemporary biblical scholarship in all its diversity, and addresses the hermeneutical issues involved. The Commission is to be congratulated for setting out its opinions so clearly and on the whole eirenically. It cautiously acknowledges the positive aspects of the various approaches, even those of liberation and feminist exegesis. Both bring useful insights to our understanding of the text, but predictably, there are difficulties in so far as they either highlight the option for the poor to the exclusion of other aspects of the biblical message, or challenge male dominance in the church by attempting to reconstruct the history of women who 'have been written out' of the biblical narrative (63–9). In particular the Instruction stresses the ecclesial nature and theological concerns of Catholic biblical interpretation. All members of the church have a role to play in the interpretation of Scripture (98) – an interesting contrast to the *Catechism's* approach – and the magisterium's role is 'to guarantee the authenticity of interpretation' and on occasion to point out instances where a particular interpretation is 'incompatible with the authentic gospel' (101).

Despite these encouraging comments, the document in the end fails to develop an adequate theory of what constitutes a theological interpretation of the Bible. In particular in dealing with the issue of presuppositions there appears to be some confusion. Catholic exegetes, we are told, must bring to their task 'presuppositions based on the certainty of faith' influenced by the work of systematic theologians (107). Yet another formulation calls for a 'pre-understanding which holds closely together modern scientific culture and the religious tradition emanating from Israel and the early Church' (85). There is an apologetic ring to both statements which do not take seriously either the idea of theology as 'faith *seeking* understanding', or the fact that biblical faith may well be at odds with modern secular culture and should provide a critical variant to what has been deemed 'progress' in our world.

A truly theological and ecclesial interpretation, which at the same time is true to the principles of the historical-critical method, must begin by taking seriously the radical plurality of the early Christian experience, not just the rather vague 'a certain pluralism' (92) which the Instruction allows for. It will seek to understand the factors that gave rise to that plurality, both within the matrix of early Christianity itself, namely, Second Temple Judaism, and within the new movement as it sought to inculturate itself within the Mediterranean and Near Eastern worlds. As well as the different faith articulations, memories and life-styles that are recorded in the New Testament writings, it will also attend to the socio-economic factors at work, recognizing that in pre-industrial societies, faith and culture cannot be separated as in our secularized Western world. Equally, in dealing with the writings of the Hebrew Bible it will be aware that diversity was also part of the Israelite and Jewish experience. Typological or christological interpretation of these writings, which the Instruction advocates, must be carefully controlled if the anti-Jewish bias of patristic exegesis is to be avoided. Within the broader context of inner-biblical exegesis, a variety of applications and midrashic developments were employed which did not necessarily to a New Testament fulfilment of those texts.

By definition, systematic theology attempts to impose/discover a unity on what is, historically and culturally, a diverse body of literature, which only finally achieved the status of 'canonical' in the third century CE. A centralized and highly institutionalized organization such as the Roman Catholic Church prefers systems to a more intangible sense of unity in diversity, which is what the biblical canon attests. Inevitably, therefore, there are real tensions between a theological system narrowly defined and critical biblical exegesis. But this need not necessarily be deplored, nor does it mean that biblical exegetes who resist such use of the Bible are either anti-theological or anti-ecclesial. The fact that all systems are themselves human constructions based on particular philosophical assumptions – Platonic, Aristotelian, Hegelian – should already alert us to the fact that systems, like texts themselves, are not written on stone, Systems need constant revising if they are not to become fossilized, just as classic texts call for constant re-readings if their surplus of meaning is to be tapped by different generations.

What is called for, therefore, is a critical dialogue, not just between professional exegetes and theologians, but also with those who read the Bible in terms of their life-experiences of oppression and marginalization, and find there the Word of Life. The only presupposition that all should bring to that dialogue would be the conviction that this collection of texts summoned them to explore again the mystery of God's love for the world as experienced in and through history. Each would bring their own gifts of understanding and wisdom, not inhibited by the need to find a specious unity to serve the needs of a particular understanding of what constitutes 'one' and 'catholic'. The fact that under the weight of evidence produced by the historical-critical method the discipline of biblical theology has virtually disappeared should warn theologians of the reality that this body of texts cannot easily be reduced to a unified system.

Equally, however, the exegete must be conscious that these texts are first and foremost religious texts which have shaped Christian identity throughout the centuries and approach them with a sympathetic, if critical awareness. Irrespective of what can be learned by the use of other methods of exploration, the task of biblical scholars, as distinct from that of ancient historians, must surely be to explicate the religious meaning of the texts with which they deal. The voices of the poor and of women must equally be respected, not just because they may bring some new insights to the reading of ancient texts, but more importantly because they have unmasked the ideological biases with which these sacred texts themselves are written.[6]

If the symbol of the open Bible has not been fully realized in the post-conciliar church, it should also be acknowledged that much has been achieved. The biblical apostolate is active in many circles of Roman Catholicism today, often in an ecumenical context of the common search for the truth that might set us free from old animosities and suspicions. As the new millennium beckons, it is to be hoped that the official magisterium also might see itself called to that openness, performing its true role as servants of the Word rather than seeking to be its master.

Notes

1. See Robert Murray SJ, 'The Human Capacity for God, and God's Initiative', in Michael J. Walsh (ed.), *Commentary on the Catechism of the Catholic Church*, London 1994, 6–34, esp. 17f.

2. See Gabriel Daly OSA, 'Creation and Original Sin', in Walsh (ed.), *Commentary* (n.1), 82–111, especially 92–6.

3. See the commentary of Philip I. Rosato SJ, 'The Sacrament of Orders', in Walsh (ed.), *Commentary* (n.1), 303–17.

4. See Sean Freyne, *The Twelve: Disciples and Apostles. An Introduction to the Theology of the First Three Gospels*, London 1968; also 'Apostle, Apostolicity', in Alan Richardson and John Bowden (eds), *A New Dictionary of Christian Theology*, London 1983, 33–5. For an excellent recent discussion of the issue see Michael Theobald, 'Die Zukunft des kirchlichen Amtes. Neutestamentliche Perspektiven angesichts gegenwärtigen Blokaden', *Stimme der Zeit* 216, 1998, 195–208.

5. All citations are from the official English translation, Editions Paulines, Sherbrooke, Quebec, Canada.

6. See the interesting remarks by U. Luz in his Presidential Address to the Society for the Study of the New Testament: 'Kann die Bibel heute noch Grundlage für die Kirche sein? Über die Aufgabe der Exegese in einer religiös-pluralistichen Gesellschaft', *New Testament Studies* 44, 1998, 317–39.

Humanitas Christi

Joseph Moingt

A major development in christology began well before Vatican II, mainly in Protestant theology and under great pressure from problems relating to the 'historical Jesus'. Since the Council this initial thrust has continued, in Catholic theology as well; new problems have been added, for example from the perspective of atheism, or new approaches have appeared, like the perspective of narrativity. However, these changes are not formally dependent on the Council. So none of these investigations, old or new, fits into the framework of the 'unanswered questions' after Vatican II with which this issue of *Concilium* is concerned. Besides, Vatican II did not touch on christological doctrine directly, and so did not introduce any real change. However, its positions in other theological areas had direct effects on the christological approach, some joining up with and reinforcing the developments alluded to above which had originated from elsewhere, and others opening up the way to new questions. First I shall mention these interventions, but only briefly, because either they do not get to the root of the problem, or they are not relevant to my subject.

Paradoxically, it is the new boldness of the Council in confronting the anthropological, cultural or political questions of present-day individuals and societies which in my view is likely to have the most effect on christology now and in the future. However, this effect is an indirect one, since it opens up the theological problem of the *humanitas Christi* to the most specific and most serious problems of humanity today. This is the sphere on which I shall concentrate, after dealing with the other effects of Vatican II on christology.

A new style of discourse

The Council discusses Christ explicitly and at some length (relatively speaking) in only two places: at the beginning of *Lumen Gentium* (1–9), on 'the mystery of the Church', founded by Christ as the 'seed and beginning' of the kingdom of God, the 'mystical body of Christ' and 'messianic people', 'gathered by God to be the instrument of the redemption of all', and in another introductory text, that of *Dei Verbum* (2–4), which presents the revelatory function of the Word, achieved by his incarnation. These are certainly fine texts, but they do not contribute anything new – though there is a new tone, a new way of doing christology which is more pastoral and evangelical than dogmatic. Furthermore, reciprocally both pastoral theology and church preaching are given a more dogmatic and deliberately christological orientation. This effect is by no means a minor one and allows us to make the prior judgment that if Vatican II brings innovations in christology, it is not at the level of content, but of the form and style of discourse which it stimulates.

Two other points confirm this sense. The first is specific to the Constitution on Revelation. By affirming that theology has to give priority to the study of scripture, after emphasizing the unity of the two Testaments and the historical character of the Gospels (*Dei Verbum* 16, 19, 24), the Council was to make a powerful contribution towards locating christology in the sphere of the Gospel narrative and the history of salvation; in this way the transition from classic treatises on the incarnation to modern and notably narrative christology (which had already been made by Protestants) was to be confirmed definitively among Catholics. The Decree on the Training of Priests, which makes 'biblical themes' the principle for teaching dogmatic theology (16), was also to act in the same direction. Suddenly, the axis of christological reflection swung downwards from above, from the eternal Word towards the Jesus of history. This was an epistemological conversion, the specific effects of which I shall sum up shortly.

New horizons

The second point is more formally innovative, even if the Council had not foreseen where the re-reading of traditional theology would lead: this is the encouragement given to the 'ecumenical effort' perceived as a 'sign of the times' (*Unitatis redintegratio* 4). By understanding ecumenism in its proper and strict sense, this encouragement furthered the convergence of Catholic and Protestant perspectives on the christological enterprise. But it is in the broad and most extended sense of this word that the true innovation appears: the interest of the Council, from its first works onwards, in non-Christian peoples, 'related to the people of God in various ways' (*Lumen Gentium* 16), and then expressed in a specific and favourable way in non-Christian religions. They too can enter the providential 'designs of salvation', for they 'often reflect a ray of that truth which enlightens all men' (*Nostra Aetate* 1–2). This interest raises the question of the sole saving mediation of Christ in new terms.

Certainly the Decree on the Missionary Activity of the Church unambiguously affirms the urgent need to proclaim the gospel to these religions, 'although in the loving providence of God they may lead one to the true God and be a preparation for the Gospel' (*Ad Gentes* 3). However, it shows that they can serve temporarily as ways of salvation when it adds that this proclamation 'tends towards eschatological fullness' (9). Inviting the 'young churches' to a 'new examination' of the Christian tradition, testing it by the 'traditions of their peoples' (22), the Council engaged the theologians of these and other countries in an inter-religious dialogue. This could not fail to produce new christological initiatives, which indeed materialized. This topic is discussed elsewhere; I limit myself to observing that it is not alien to the humanist concern of the conciliar church, which I shall now discuss.

The christological novelty of Vatican II

Paradoxically, as I have said, to discover the true 'unanswered questions' in christology which were opened up by Vatican II, we now turn to a document which might seem to be the least theological document, since it touches on questions which no synod had deigned to touch on before it – unless one grants (and this will be my position) that it finally discovered true questions worthy of the interest of theology. For this very reason the document is truly innovative, as also because it welcomes with sympathy the 'new ideas' that the magisterium of the nineteenth century had rejected with scorn and horror. The document I wish to discuss is the 'pastoral' Constitution *Gaudium et Spes*, a text which deliberately presents itself as the charter of a Christian humanism written in brotherly 'dialogue' with the 'modern world', as the title and introduction indicate. Its intention of addressing all men and women, even atheists, taking up their questions and their anxieties 'about current trends in the world, about their place and role in the universe' – 'for it is man himself who must be saved; it is mankind that must be renewed' (3.1) – and its concern to scrutinize the 'signs of the times', which are the changes that have taken place in modern times, in order to 'interpret them in the light of the Gospel' (4.1), led the Council to put the Jesus of history at the very heart of human history. And it is here that we can discover the christological innovations brought about by this 'conversion' of the theological focus towards human questions.

The first part of this document, the only one which will occupy us, is divided into four chapters. I shall limit myself to recalling their topics: having exalted 'the dignity of the human person' and then shown its interest in promoting 'human community', the Council appeals to revelation 'to clarify the course upon which man has just entered' 'by his mind and his work' (33), the autonomy of which it affirms (36). And it ends by offering the help of the church to human activity and society, recognizing what it has itself received from the world and its cultures in the course of time.

At each stage of this course the Council presents an appropriate aspect of the face of Christ: 'the new Adam, (who) fully reveals man to himself and brings to light his most high calling' (22.1) – 'the Word made flesh (who) willed to share in human fellowship (32.2) – 'a perfect man, he entered world history, taking that history into himself and recapitulating it' (38.3), so that already 'here on earth the kingdom is mysteriously present' (39.3) – 'The Lord (who) is the goal of human history, the focal point of the desires of history and civilization, the centre of mankind' (45.2).

Absolutely classic, and even more precisely 'from above', this christo-logy, simply by being projected on to the historicity of the world, in the worldliness of history, by virtue of its goal of serving as the foundation for a humanism in accordance with the gospel, promises new and more decisive shifts, which I shall now sketch out.

Jesus in the shadow of unbelief

The new look which the church of the twentieth century directed towards so many humanistic values which it had rejected less than half a century previously – the recognition of the dignity of the human person, its intelligence, moral conscience and freedom, despite the pretensions of its reason, its claims to a moral authority and the boldness of its concern for liberation – led it to discover that 'atheism is one of the most serious problems of our time, and one that deserves more thorough treatment' (*Gaudium et Spes* 19.1), since it derives from a 'desire for autonomy', taken to such a degree 'as to object to any dependence on God at all' (20.1). We get the impression (perhaps pushing it a bit) that the fathers of Vatican II are repeating the analysis which led Dietrich Bonhoeffer in his prison to note – and to accept – that a powerful and irresistible ground-swell was leading humankind, from the first sparks of modernity on, to depart from the native shores of religion.

But does the Council accept this *fact* of a generalized unbelief as a methodological preamble and horizon for the discussion which it wants to have on this world? By qualifying it as systematic atheism (20.1) which has to be rejected (21.1), it rules out any possibility of regarding this desire for autonomy as the free unfolding of human rationality in its proper space – a legitimate expansion, even if it drives back beliefs which were provisionally installed there (Bonhoeffer's 'God of the gaps'). By appealing immediately to the mystery of the incarnate Word to illuminate the human word (22.1), it manifests a haste which does not respect this autonomy, *a priori* projecting human truth outside its natural and worldly condition.

However, the research of the Council drives us to go further than it has gone itself. Its desire to exalt human dignity invites us to recognize it in the limits of the human condition before interrogating revelation about the mystery of the human vocation (19.1; 22.6). And when the Council wrote that 'by his incarnation, he, the Son of God, in a certain way united himself with each man', working, thinking, loving, with human hands and a human intelligence, will and heart (22.2), it suggested that to speak of Christ to people so remote from religious language, it is necessary to go through Christ's humanity in all its density before wanting to go beyond it and to have Christ presented to them in the very first approach in a language which they can understand naturally: not a language of mysteries but a language of humanity, starting from reason.

Thus Spinoza once praised Christ for addressing men of all countries and all times in the language of common reason, and Bonhoeffer, quite close to our time, explored a 'non-religious' language for stating the identity of Jesus to our contemporaries, calling Jesus 'the man for others'. When one has accepted that this world has ceased to be religious (despite whatever degree of religion it has been able to preserve), one feels the need for a new language, at least new prolegomena, to open it up for the gospel. To set out on his way is to go well beyond a preamble to a christology either from below or from above; it is to erect the humanity of Jesus as a working hypothesis in this sense: not to seek to show that the truth of this individual is that he is God, which amounts to diminishing and dissimulating his humanity, but to seek to show that he is fully human, the man for all, the one in whom we can recognize and *do* our truth as human beings in this world. Such a concern brings about a turning point in the course of christology: this man shows himself to be Son of God when his humanity allows him to be grasped as the revelation of the humanity of God.

Christ down history

Calling men and women to think and act in accordance with their social nature, to 'promote the common good of all the human family' (26.1) to the point of 'making ourselves the neighbours of everyone, no matter who they are' (27.2), and 'to take part in common enterprises' (31.3), the Council gives them the example of the incarnate Word, who 'in person willed to share in human fellowship' (32.2). But how did he come to share it, if not through a shared history? Not only by means of activities freely accepted, but also by the *constraint* of a birth which gave him a place in the chain of generations.

The Council was right to perceive that in order to interest human beings who had come of age and were subjects of their history, it had to show them at what point he was linked up, not only with human nature but also with human history. However, it continues to speak the patristic language of condescension, which proclaims that the Son of God humbled himself in order to enter into time, without losing any of the privileges of his eternity. For it fails to reflect that one does not enter history from outside, by an act of benevolence, but becomes human by the very fact of owing one's origin to a history which has us born into the human world. The generosity does not replace the *genus*. Historicity is the native condition of the human person, just as temporality is inherent in human nature understood as being-in-the-world. History is received passively as a heritage before one is freely taken up in it, in such a way that it becomes a task to fulfil. For better or worse, one enters into a solidarity with the history which precedes us before it becomes that which we work to build with those who bear the same yoke. In short, solidarity is prescribed and not invented.

In the case of Jesus, the discourse of solidarity requires us to resort to the narrative of his genealogy, which traces back his divine sonship, as a vocation to honour, in a chain of generations at the end of which he is recognized to be 'son of Adam, son of God' (Luke 3.38). The Nicene Creed makes him follow an opposite course, from heaven to earth, from eternity to time. However, there is no other way of making *conceivable* the solidarity of Jesus with human history than to recognize that he is a tributary of (and has to pay tribute to) our old history. The solidarity of the Son of God with us – his kenosis – is not that he *humbles* himself to the point of bearing a destiny to which he would not have been constrained by necessity of his birth; he can only emerge from the same *humus* as that from which all his fellow Jews emerged.

Dogmatic discourse about the incarnation ended up forgetting that the Son of God, coming from God to us 'in the fullness of time', also had to go by way of history. The discourse of Vatican II, by its internal logic, shows the new demands of the incarnation on the side of humanity, which were ignored by dogma. According to modern anthropology it is 'the patience of history' – chance or initiative? – which brings Jesus 'into human fellowship'. The Son begins his kenosis not by stripping himself, but by taking up links which no one can bear unless chained in advance by destiny. The new Adam has to be born loaded with the centuries of the old Adam, as his genealogy recounts. The discourse of solidarity refers christology back to the story of the humanity of Jesus before it can celebrate his eternal origin.

Jesus under the horizon of the kingdom of God

Moving from society to the whole of the activities involved in its progress, the constitution *Gaudium et Spes* recognizes that 'the demand for autonomy is perfectly in order' (36.2) and offers to 'the human family' the help of Christ to 'establish a universal brotherhood', to 'improve the circumstances of daily life' and to lead 'free men towards the future' (38.1). Different though it will be from the present world, the expectation of this future should not distract anyone from working towards earthly progress, which 'is of vital concern to the kingdom of God, in so far as it can contribute to the better ordering of human society' (39.2). All these activities 'we will find once again', since 'here on earth the kingdom is mysteriously present' (39.3), the active nucleus of the 'transformation of the cosmos' to come (39.1).

It is worth emphasizing in this argument the concern of the Council to put an end to the traditional and ruinous separation between the spiritual and the temporal and to affirm, while maintaining their distinction, the total 'penetration of the earthly and the heavenly city' (40.3), the principle of which is Christ, in that 'a perfect man, he entered world history, taking that history into himself and recapitulating it' (38.1). This new vision of the mystery of the world open to the presence of the kingdom of God calls for going beyond the formula of Chalcedon, as was desired by Karl Rahner, since this is always in danger of removing the humanity of Christ from a world to which he does not seem to have the same attachments as ours. In fact, if Christians feel themselves too often torn between their vocation as believers and their obligations as citizens of the world, between their 'yearning for the world to come' and the 'earthly service of men' (38.1), is not the fundamental reason that they hesitate to recognize completely the Christ as 'one of us and like to us in all things' (22.2), since his personal link with the world does not appear the same as ours?

Men and women of (post-)modernity are more strongly aware than the ancients that their humanity is identical with their 'worldliness'. They are not beings thrown on the earth and provided with a superior essence; endowed with vision, perception, thought and language, they are beings of the world which is seen, perceived, thought and expressed in them. All that they are is given to them by the world, and it is this participation in the being of the world which constitutes their intercommunication and humanity. According to this new understanding of itself, the humanity of the incarnate Word is not defined solely at the level of our abstract substance, but equally in connection with our bond to the world, the supreme reality of which is to be a shared origin. It cannot consist simply in 'taking our substance'; it is received from the history of the world, where it is prepared this side of the incarnation. Thus the 'interpenetration' of the kingdom and the world affirmed by the Council claims to be based on a new perception of the being of Christ: no longer just of the 'mode of union' between the Word and humanity, but of the union of his humanity to the being of the world in which the common being of humankind is shaped.

The reign of Christ against the horizon of the world

Other conclusions for christology could be drawn from the reflections in *Gaudium et Spes* on 'human activity in the universe'. They can also be drawn from the chapter which concludes all its reflections on this subject, discussing the church 'in the world and its life and activity there' (40.1). Persuaded that 'whoever follows Christ the perfect man becomes himself more a man' (41.1), the church offers its help in unifying the human family and strengthening its institutions (42.4–5), and exhorts its faithful to shun any 'divorce' between their faith and their earthly activities (43.1). Recognizing all that it has received and can still receive from history, cultures and human institutions, it desires to establish a 'living exchange' between itself and the world (44.2) until the coming of the Saviour, 'the goal of human history, the focal point of the desires of history and civilization' (45.2).

This conclusion takes christology further down the way opened up by the previous reflections. Here it is a matter of applying to the action of the Christ the insights that have been gained about his person, in order to avoid any dichotomy between his activities. So much emphasis has been put on Christ's action in the 'supernatural' sphere, spiritual and eternal, that it has become difficult to say what contribution he makes to this world: not just to what he accomplishes beyond himself, but simply in the limitations of his spatial and temporal condition, if he is interested in this world for itself and as it is. If Christ makes 'whoever follows him more a man', has he made the world more habitable over two thousand years? And if the failure is to be blamed on those who have not followed him, what sign of the disinterested love of Christ for our world can be given to the men and women of our time?

For a long time political theology and liberation theology have been preoccupied with meeting this challenge, also referring back to Vatican II. It is not evident that the church has endorsed their efforts. At all events, to reconcile the church with the world it will not be enough to promise to the world that the world will benefit by a spin-off from those who work for another world; it is necessary to unify the activity of Christ in the direction of the kingdom more rigorously with his gratuitous interest in this world; his preaching to the sons of the kingdom more fully with his ethical message to the men and women of good will; his saving action with his cosmic plan; salvation with creation. We owe a great debt to Vatican II for making the enterprise imaginable. As a result of it we can see better the difficulties caused by a long tradition of dualistic christology.

I still have not suggested what christology could be or could not be; could say or could not say; could do or could not do, if it recognized its debt towards human history and the development of its cultures and institutions, as the Council does in a very generous and very general statement (44), in a way which could lead theologians to a more critical discernment and a more open distribution of their patrimony. I shall content myself with raising the problem, which stems more broadly from the theology of revelation and tradition, and which will certainly be a task for tomorrow's theologians – but those of today are well aware of it. From Vatican II I retain the precious assurance that if Christians become more human the more they follow Christ, then reciprocally, the more Christ is shown in his humanity, the closer he is brought to the world which he has come to save. The dogma of the incarnation is constructed by proclaiming that we must not be ashamed of the *humanitates*, the passivities, the sufferings, the infirmities of Christ: of all the things in which he is like us, including our deficiencies. The tradition of the church, handed down by Vatican II, thus encourages us to explore the *humanitas Christi*.

Translated by John Bowden

The Wealth of Gifts of the Spirit and their Christian Identity

Jürgen Moltmann

In this article I want to discuss the Christian identity of the multiplicity of the gifts of the Spirit and the spiritual multiplicity of Christian identity. A whole series of unanswered questions lies hidden here, relating both to the government of the church and to Christianity in the world.

I

Christianity came into being in an exuberant springtime in which gifts of the Spirit were experienced. What happened to the apostles at Pentecost and after that to the Christian communities, wherever they arose, could only be interpreted as the fulfilment of the promise in Joel of the eschatological 'outpouring of the Spirit of God upon flesh' (Joel 3.1–5; Acts 2).[1] 'Sons and daughters', 'manservants and maidservants' and the 'old men' are the first to experience the advent of the Spirit. They prophesy and have 'visions and dreams'. But the flood of the Spirit will come upon 'all flesh', i.e. all living beings. In the dawn of this universal outpouring of the spirit a new equality of the sexes (sons and daughters), a new equality of the generations (old and young), and a new social equality (manservants and maidservants) come into being. This spirit-filled community attests to 'all flesh' deliverance in the eschatological danger: 'the sun will turn into darkness and the moon into blood'. The community which confesses Christ as Lord and believes in the God who has raised him from the dead is the place for the manifestation of this overflowing abundance of powers of the Spirit, as Paul always emphasizes.[2]

The identity in the multiplicity of charisms lies in the confession of Christ, for the presence of the risen Christ arouses the 'powers of the world to come', the term used by the Letter to the Hebrews for the gifts of the Spirit (6.5). But the inexhaustible origin of the gifts of the Spirit also lies in the notion of the resurrection. There is that Christian identity only in the multiplicity of the Spirit, just as there is this multiplicity of the Spirit only in Christian identity. Paul emphasizes the unity in this situation, which is charismatically so rich: 'There are all kinds of gifts, but there is one Spirit. There are all kinds of callings, but there is one Lord. There are all kinds of powers, but there is one God, who accomplishes all things in all' (I Cor.12.4–6). Manifestly this is not a monarchical unity but a trinitarian unity of Spirit – Christ – God, which embraces gifts – callings – powers. Therefore Paul adds as a further definition of unity the building up of the community: 'In each are manifested the gifts of the Spirit to the common good' (12.7). He uses the image of the many members of the one body and the one body of the many members to say that all, with their gifts of the Spirit which are so different, are dependent on one another; that they are held together in their multiplicity through love; that they suffer together and rejoice together, and finally owe the weakest members the greatest respect, because this is the body of the crucified Lord. So the unity of the charismatic body of Christ does not lie in one member, but in the fellowship of different members.[3] Not even the apostles stand at the head, but the 'one Spirit', by which all 'are baptized into one body', and are equal and free (I Cor.12.13; Gal.3.28).

The fellowship of this multiplicity of those endowed with the Spirit is also shown in their liturgical assemblies: 'When you come together, each one has a hymn, a lesson, a revelation, a tongue or an interpretation. Let all things be done for edification (viz., of the community)' (I Cor.14.26). There is no question here of a hierarchical order which distinguishes between priests and laity, for 'God is not a God of subordination but of peace' (14.33), and this peace is won and preserved only through love. The 'mission and expansion of Christianity', to cite the title of Adolf von Harnack's famous book, was brought about in the first centuries by Christians filled with the Spirit: women and men, slaves and free, poor and rich; and by the formation of communities in which each individual was accepted and used with the individuality of his or her special powers. Every revival, reform or reformation movement in the history of the Christian church has experienced something of this charismatic spring of early Christianity and introduced it into church and society: the confession of Christ and faith in the God who raises from the dead; fellowship in the colourful multiplicity of the powers of the spirit; shared preaching in many forms, especially by women; experiences of healing, speaking in tongues, the concern for freedom.[4]

Existing churches which do not allow this freedom and multiplicity of the gifts of the Spirit 'quench' and 'disturb' the Holy Spirit and get in the way of its callings. They become petrified and impoverished in their existing order.

II

I now want to investigate more closely the Christian identity which not only allows such a multiplicity of powers of the Spirit, but also sets them free and brings them about.

The identity which individuals and communities find in Christ through faith is manifestly not a closed, aggressive identity, of the kind that comes into being in friend-foe relationships, but an open, inviting, accepting and saving identity. In it people not only come to themselves but also go out from themselves; they are not only gathered but also sent. This is an identity which comes into being in the movement from the one to the many. Therefore it is not a static identity of which one could say 'Semper idem', 'Always the same', but an identity of process which comes into being in the process of the outpouring of the Spirit 'on all flesh'. Any personal identity in faith in Christ 'transcends' itself in hope for the coming kingdom of Christ; any group identity in particular communities 'transcends' its own limits in the direction of 'all flesh'. The gifts of the Spirit are not only given in an introverted way for building up the community but also set free as 'powers of the world to come' (Heb.6.5), to renew the whole suffering creation, so that 'all flesh' may come alive. In this respect Christian identity is an identity which transcends itself.

Therefore Christian identity conceals in itself a deep non-identity: in faith in Christ the believer receives a new identity which is symbolized by the giving of the name in baptism; 'in Christ' he or she is 'a new creation' (II Cor.5.17) and is 'born anew' from the Spirit (John 3.3). The new creation of all things which Christ will complete in his day is already manifest in the believers. Therefore at the same time 'the life' of believers is still 'hidden with Christ in God'. It will 'be revealed' only in the parousia of Christ in glory (Col.3.3). We can call that the eschatological non-identity of believers in Christ.[5] In this respect they are not only 'of the world' but are also themselves still 'hidden': *homo absconditus in Christo* (Augustine, *Confessions* X, 17). In Christ they have become a mystery to themselves which is waiting for Christ's revelation, for the 'unveiled face'. This hiddenness of the believers escapes any political, social and official church identification by which otherwise it could be controlled like everything else that can be identified and established. This hiddenness relativizes and volatilizes all existing fixed points.

III

If we go on to consider the abundant multiplicity of the gifts of the Spirit, we must not only think of an 'ordered' multiplicity but also ask about the origin of the Spirit and its powers. Is it the Spirit of God, the Spirit of Christ or the God of the Spirit?[6]

In the Old Testament there is mention only of the Spirit of God, by which 'the Lord' works what he wills. According to the Synoptic Gospels the Spirit of God comes down upon Jesus through his baptism and 'rests' upon him. In the life and activity of the earthly Jesus the Spirit of God is the real subject. That is the element of truth in any Spirit christology. God also acts on Jesus through his Spirit in the cross and resurrection: through the eternal Spirit Jesus surrenders himself to the point of death (Heb.9.14); through the Spirit God raises him from the dead (Rom.8.11); Jesus is present now as the 'life-giving Spirit' (I Cor.15.45). But according to the Gospel of John, it is the Risen Christ who sends the Holy Spirit (John 20.22). He sends him from the Father (John 15.26), for the Spirit proceeds from the Father. Only on the basis of the resurrection and exaltation of Jesus Christ is it possible in Christianity to speak not only of the Spirit of God but also of the Spirit of Christ, and theologically to develop a christological pneumatology. The unity of the origin of the Spirit and his gifts, which is differentiated into God and Christ or Father and Son, can, however, remain. It is not good to use the *filioque* in the creed of the Western church to put the Spirit in third place and thus speak of the Spirit of God only in the form of the Spirit of Christ, as is stated by the sequence 'the Father – through the Son – in the Holy Spirit'.[7] For then the Spirit is one-sidedly bound up with Christ and the church's representation of Christ: the Spirit as the subjective effect of the objective word and sacrament of Christ communicated only through the 'spiritual office' of the community of the 'laity'. The logic of the *filioque* has led to an ecclesiasticization of the Holy Spirit and his powers and effects. If we leave it out, then in addition to the series mentioned above, 'Father – Son – Spirit', there is also the other possibility of 'Father – Spirit – Son', and we are led through the Son to the Spirit of God who is already at work everywhere in the community of creation. The Spirit of Christ at work in the community of Christ is then so to speak the first wave of the energies of the Spirit of God which are pouring themselves out upon all flesh. Then, not least, the God of the Spirit takes on a significance relatively independent of God the Father and God the Son, as the 'Spirit of truth' and the eternal Light. Only a pneumatology deployed in trinitarian fashion allows us to perceive the whole wealth of the powers of the Spirit and preserves us from suppressing them. The powers of the Spirit are not 'supernatural' gifts by comparison with those that are named 'natural'; they are not 'within the church' as opposed to being in 'the world'; they are not 'other-worldly' as opposed to what is this-worldly; they are not spiritual or religious as opposed to the powers of the body. They are the universal powers of the God who creates, redeems and heals. As powers of the new creation of all things, they are to be understood as the 'beginning and pledge' of the coming glory of the triune God.

IV

That brings us, finally, to the difficult question of a criterion for discerning the spirits or powers of the Spirit. The ecclesiological criterion of the existing church is relatively simple, but all the more questionable. Pope John Paul II recently imposed the obligation of 'obedience to the bishops' on an assembly of charismatic groups. As the bishops are obedient to the pope, who represents the existing church teaching, the link to the tradition is clear. Thus innovative reforms of the life and teaching of the church are almost inconceivable: its dogmatic statements are infallible and irreformable.[8] The Protestant criterion of scripture is rather more difficult; according to this, 'scriptural' doctrines are distinguished from those which contradict scripture. This presupposes an infallible authority of scripture which can hardly be sustained in the age and cultural sphere of historical-critical research; nor does it do justice to the Reformation, which arrived at the authority of scripture – sola scriptura – from the content of scripture – solus Christus.[9] Criteria then arise in the hermeneutical circle of the exegesis of scripture by scripture. The christological criterion of the name of Jesus and the sign of the cross works best.[10] In exorcism the evil spirits are driven out by invocation of the name of Christ and the sign of the cross. What applies negatively to exorcism applies positively to the knowledge of the Holy Spirit. What can stand in the face of the crucified Christ is of God; what contradicts him is not. What serves discipleship of Jesus comes from the living power of the Holy Spirit; what contradicts it comes from the powers of the Evil One and death. For discipleship of Jesus and life in the Spirit are two sides of the same way. But with such criteria, do we do justice to the eternal origin of the powers, gifts and callings of God, the holy Spirit? At any rate it is better to raise such unanswered questions than to repress them with obedience towards 'infallible' authorities.

Translated by John Bowden

Notes

1. Y. Congar, *I Believe in the Holy Spirit* (3 vols), London 1983; J. Moltmann, *The Spirit of Life. A Universal Affirmation*, London and Minneapolis 1992; M. Welker, *Gottes Geist. Theologie des Heiligen Geistes*, Neukirchen 1992.

2. J. D. G. Dunn, *Jesus and the Spirit. A Study of the Religious and Charismatic Experience of Jesus and the First Christians as reflected in the New Testament*, London and Philadelphia 1977.

3. E. Käsemann, 'Ministry and Community in the New Testament', in *Essays on New Testament Themes*, London 1964, 63–94.

4. See W. J. Hollenweger, *The Pentecostals*, London 1972; D. Martin, *Tongues of Fire. The Explosion of Protestantism in Latin America*, Oxford 1990.

5. J. Moltmann, *Der verborgene Mensch*, Wuppertal 1961.

6. For this distinction and the ecumenical discussion of it cf. *L. Vischer* (ed.), *Geist Gottes – Geist Christi. Ökumenische Überlegungen zur Filioque Kontroverse*, Frankfurt 1981.

7. See the detailed discussion in J. Moltmann, *The Trinity and the Kingdom of God,* London 1981.

8. Thus also now the papal ordinance *Ad tuendam fidem* (1998), with which Catholic theologians have to promise 'obedience to definitively defined truths'.

9. H. Diem, *Was heisst schriftgemass?*, Neukirchen 1958.

10. J. Moltmann, *The Source of Life. The Holy Spirit and the Theology of Life*, London and Minneapolis 1997, 17f.

Whose God is God? The View of the Victims

Dietmar Mieth and Christoph Theobald

God is certainly no one's property, but God does give himself. In this special sense we can ask, 'To whom does God belong? Whose God is God?' To answer 'God belongs to no one but himself' or 'God belongs to all' would be as problematical as to answer the question 'Where is God?' either with the naive notion 'God is in heaven', or the meaningless formula 'God is everywhere and nowhere'.

God is an Other, but God is not other. '*Alius non aliud*' was the way in which Meister Eckhart and Nicholas of Cusa put it. So God cannot be put at a completely abstract distance, though it would be wrong to want to get hold of God in inappropriate reifications. In addition to the question about where God is and to whom God belongs, a third example can be introduced here: God is neither woman nor man. But if one then clothes abstract deity in the usual male terms for the abstract ('man', etc.), the abstraction becomes sexist, and retouching the abstract becomes hypocrisy.

If we reject wrong abstractions – there are indeed also right abstractions –, we are directed towards a concrete entity which is 'in possession': the church. Is not God the God of the church, which expounds the divine messages and the divine laws? Is not the church the place of sacramental binding and loosing, by which God binds himself? It cannot be denied that as one goes higher in the church, one encounters such notions, spoken and unspoken. But even if God does not claim any abstract and therefore meaningless sovereignty over the church, to what degree is the church not also bound to God's sovereign giving of himself in possession, which is clearly mediated through Jesus of Nazareth in the footsteps of the prophets? God is the God of the poor, those without rights, the humiliated, the vulnerable and the disadvantaged – in short, the victims.

If God makes a concrete disclosure of himself and given himself in this sense in the human world 'from below', in cries from the deep, then we can ask a twofold question – in the context of the unanswered questions.

First, does the church see God primarily where he manifests his Spirit, where the brotherly and sisterly relationship with his Son (according to Matt.25) is not only reflected in the face of the other but actually in this face? Or does it locate the possession of God which it claims elsewhere in its words and actions? If it did, the church would constantly be threatened with the charge of idolatry, because it puts God in the wrong place on earth and claims that God is massively present where he is only weakly reflected, whereas his hidden, feeble presence in the depths only finds powerless words with which to communicate.

The second question is just as important: if it is claimed that God is the God of the victims, how can this be recognized? Or does it remain the 'rock of atheism' (as Büchner put it) that there are no proofs of the spirit and of power in these depths of misery? We know this question as the theodicy question, and it has no answer, because all attempts at an answer would have to put a theological system above the God who gives himself. For if we seek to disclose theologically the manifest impotence of God in his own party, among the victims, we call it either the 'price of freedom' or the 'price of love'; in other words, we subject God to the systematic constraint of a faithfulness to himself which has previously been conceptually domesticated. That is understandable and in a sense unavoidable, but it does not resolve the 'mystery of evil', because the inappropriateness of our theological discourse is expressed here in a special way.

Our concern here is merely to raise the unanswered question correctly, to avoid over-hasty solutions and not to deny how in the face of the theodicy question faith has to walk a tightrope. Here we first of all have to note that in our time the victims are more tangibly, comprehensively and urgently present than ever before – and this very permanence of their vivid presence dulls us and makes us indifferent. This is our way of making the intolerable tolerable through customary mechanisms of suppression. We need not state this as a reproach; we can also say it in a way which expresses pity for human weakness: we cannot watch one hour with the one who attempts to give an answer to the fate of the victims by entering into their godforsakenness. This event does not remain abstract; as what Hegel called a 'speculative Good Friday', it is too remote and exalted; it is the response of unyielding practical solidarity in the face of the failure of any attempts at rescue, liberation and redemption which appear as power: these always create more problems of misery than they solve. Here God's giving of himself in possession is maintained to the point that it is endured to the death. Criticism of such theologies of sacrifice is more than justified: what kind of an image of God do they have? The way in which the Old Testament sacrifice of Isaac is taken up inevitably shows that God intervenes for the sacrifice and thus prejudices the prophetic 'mercy not sacrifice'.

But how do the victims benefit from God sharing their ravaged face and suffering their own incapacity to answer? They have a promise. However, this promise would be mere consolation, were not the divine solidarity one which abides and which can be renewed in the faith of those who are obedient to God. This needs further explanation. It can be a help to distinguish between pro-solidarity and con-solidarity. Those who practise pro-solidarity do not share the fate of those with whom they are in solidarity. Only those who practice con-solidarity enter into the same event, and cannot avoid so doing. Here the very thing that cannot be avoided without restricting redemption is paradoxically what re-deems. There are signs of this in the living church, among Christians who are steeped with faith. God is in this practical place. There God has made himself obedient (the picture of the one who is in the form of a servant, in Isaiah and Paul). Therefore the theodicy question is not a game which can be solved by systematic theology but a practical question, a question to the church and a question to individual forms of faith. In both cases the question remains open like a wound which will not heal. And it is better to be disturbed and destroyed by this challenge as 'only' someone who is in con-solidarity, or similarly to have one's usual order threatened as being 'only' a church which is in con-solidarity, than to give way to the powerful capacity of our minds to shed concerns, to build up apparatuses which divert us from the central existence of our faith.

But how can we speak from the perspective of the victims anyway? In this issue we hear their voices only weakly in some contributions, corresponding to our own weaknesses. This too belongs with the unanswered questions: how do we make it possible to hear dumb voices, to make visible the faceless, to feel the unfelt?

Translated by John Bowden

Bibliography

R. Ammicht-Quinn, *Von Lissabon bis Auschwitz. Zum Paradigmawechsel in der Theodizeefrage*, Studien zur Theologischer Ethik 43, Fribourg and Freiburg 1992
J. B. Metz, 'Memoria passionis, Un incoraggiamento alle responsabilità universale', in D. Mieth, E. Schillebeeckx and H. Snijdewind (eds), *Cammino e Visione*, Brescia 1996, 179–84.

A New Way of Being Christians. Preparing to Encounter Neighbours of Other Faiths

Felix Wilfred

Theology of religions has come to occupy a very central place in contemporary debates, with christology as its fulcrum. We are in the face of an unanswered question that has raised much dust. But in the course of the new century, I surmise that the terms of the present-day discussion will cease to be particularly exciting, and pass on in history as one more theological controversy – say between inclusivism and pluralism, absolutism and relativism, christocentrism and theocentrism and so on. We need only recall how tempestuously the question whether there is salvation outside the church was discussed, and that was not long ago. Issues of this kind are bound to slide into the limbo of oblivion, very much like the many heated controversies that divided the theological fraternity through the centuries such as icons and non-icons, freedom and grace, natural and supernatural, monogenism and polygenism, etc.

These questions are superseded, not because undisputed solutions have been arrived at in every case – far from it – but simply because the site of the theological discourse has shifted to new grounds. Besides, such questions are historically and culturally so loaded with presuppositions that when they are moved lock, stock and barrel to other cultural and linguistic worlds, answering them could prove as embarrassing as yes or no to a question saying 'Have you stopped taking drugs?'

Of course, by saying all this we have not laid to rest the reality of our relationships with peoples of other religious traditions. When the sound and fury of the raging theological debates wane and recede, we will be still left face to face with our neighbours, relationships with whom are of no small importance for us. We are, and will increasingly be, confronted by the fundamental question of being Christians in a world of religious experiences other than ours. We perhaps entertain the thought today that we have answered the questions arising out of the new situation, simply because we manage to produce ingenious theological constructs to squeeze in (leading to serious deformation almost beyond recognition!) what has been unfamiliar to us.

The great challenge we are going to face in the new century is to develop a new way of being Christians resulting from our new relationships with our neighbours of other faiths. This encounter calls for honest and serious preparation on our part. In terms of method and attitude, it does not imply that we make light of, much less abandon, our legitimate confessional or faith-approach. Far from it. But it does call for surmounting the insular mentality and overcoming the fear-psychosis that make us believe that other religions around us are like 'roaring lions' (cf. I Peter 5.8) circumambulating only to devour our Christian identity.

As part of the preparation for our future encounter with the religious world of our neighbours, I would highlight in this brief contribution just three important tasks:[1] I. To rethink our conception of what is meant by universal and recast it in a spiritual mould; II. To promote a culture of tolerance and peace; III. To baptize our prevailing theologies in the mystical stream.

I. Universality welling up from spirituality

Is not our dominant conception of universality very much conditioned by the mediaeval experience and the historical vicissitudes of the nineteenth century? At a time when the travesty of universality is the order of the day, and when the ubiquitous is being paraded as the universal, it is clear why Christian witness and practice today should offer a more gospel-inspired understanding of universality in the relationship with followers of other religious traditions. The difficulty is not so much the Christian claim of universality as the nature of the universality being presupposed. The gospel-universality is something conspicuously spiritual; it is the universality of God's overwhelming grace. On the other hand, it is something that links up with the endless openness and transcendence of the human spirit in communion with the infinite mystery. The message of Jesus and the mystery of his person offer us a deeply spiritual, grace-based and refreshingly new approach to universality. It is a universality that does not isolate Christians, but relates them in dialogical encounter with neighbours of other faiths.

Today we require a kenotic and non-hegemonic universality that will enable us to forge fresh and respectful relationships with our neighbours of other faiths. Its openness and outreach will be fascinating, and obviously call for a different set of values and attitudes which mirror more closely the spirit of the Gospel and of Jesus. It is a universality that is transparent and sincere, elevating, transforming and liberating, free as it is from any hegemonic power-agenda. This needs to be said because a merely formalistic type of universality, at whatever level, has an irresistible temptation to dominate and manipulate.[2] Such a universal – even if it is a contradiction in terms – can only be designated as a 'parochial universal'.

Universality of the mind could become a means of colonization and control, whereas the universality of the Spirit is of untrammelled freedom. The gospel universality of the kingdom is that of the Spirit. It is compared to a tree on which all kinds of birds come and rest (Matt. 13.32). It is a universality of communion as in a banquet in which people from east and west, north and south, come and partake of the meal (Luke 13.29). We are in the face of a universality that wells up from within and like a mighty river surging overflows its institutional banks to reach out and commune with the beyond in a spirit of affinity. Such images and narratives of the universal can lead us to a new way of being Christians, and at the same time speak to our neighbours of other faiths and strike a chord of resonance in their hearts and minds.

II. Promoting a culture of tolerance and peace

Let us start admitting that there are limits to tolerance; that there is the danger of indifferentism lurking in it; that one may end up by assuming the attitude of 'anything goes'. Having said that, however, in the multi-religious context of today we need to recognize that tolerance is essential for the very survival of the human family; that it has great potential to the universality for witnessing of the gospel. Tolerance is not a weakness. It is only as much weakness as showing the right cheek to someone who slaps you on the left (Matt. 5.39). Such an attitude and pattern of behaviour can stem only from a deep spiritual experience and mental frame of wisdom. And it may not be intelligible to those who have not attempted to enter into the interior depths and contemplate the Sermon on the Mount in them. All this is reason enough why the Christian relationship to other faiths needs to be inspired by an evangelical spirit of tolerance and peace. If we do not want to end up repeating the ways of *compelle intrare* ('compel them to come in', with reference to Luke 14.23), with all its unfortunate consequences, in future we need to live and practise tolerance as an expression of true Christian universality.

There is another reason for practising tolerance: the ultimate judgment is reserved to God and that cannot be usurped by human beings, however high and enlightened they may consider themselves to be. This point is well illustrated by the parable of the wheat and the weeds (Matt. 13.24 – 30). Further, we need to recognize that in our human and societal relationships as well as in our understanding – which also includes religions – we cannot always deal in black-and-white terms;[3] there is something like a grey zone. Otherwise it would mean that every difference and otherness, any lack of clarity and distinctness (*pace* Descartes), is a motive for conflict and violence, physical or moral. It is a perilous proposition that peace can be achieved only when we arrive at clarity and certainty. We need to cultivate this spirit of tolerance and peace continuously in our Christian communities and bring it to bear upon our relationship with other faiths.

Interestingly, tolerance has become a meeting point between the spirit of Asian cultural heritage and the exigencies of postmodernity.[4] The traditional Asian cultures have been very much attuned to a life of integration and harmony, giving rise to a way of life which on the whole is very much marked by respect and tolerance towards the religious experiences, beliefs and practices of the other.[5] On the other hand, tolerance has been an important issue raised by modernity, the other being the autonomy of temporal realities. Whereas the issue of autonomy of temporal realities has been addressed, though belatedly, in the last few decades, the question of tolerance has not been faced in its practical consequences for life, even though in principle the right of religious liberty has been acknowledged. If the future is going to be one of multi-religious societies – as is becoming more and more evident – it is important that we face squarely this question raised by modernity as a matter of daily life. In such a context, the cultivation of evangelical tolerance will be a Christian response to the Asian cultures, and at the same time it will be also a response to an unanswered question raided by modernity and sharpened in these postmodern times.

Furthermore, Christian faith-claims of universality cannot be at the expense of accountability to contemporary society in terms of tolerance and peace. In fact, the United Nations has declared the year 2000 the year of the culture of peace. Christian communities need to be seasoned by a culture of peace – so very much an essential part of the gospel – to be able to encounter the religious world of the neighbours. Any intolerance of tolerance will raise questions about the credibility of the universality being claimed and its spiritual quality. This is also very important in view of the history of mission which, as we know, was not always the most elevating example of the evangelical spirit of peace, compassion and understanding. In the new century, a fresh Christian witness of tolerance will only contribute to make the Christian faith-claim of universality credible. The two are not contradictory, as is often made out.

III. Baptizing theology in the mystical stream

For theology to be able to be of assistance to the Christian community in its encounter with peoples of other faiths, it will need to be an expression of spirituality and assume true mystical traits. This is because the spiritual and mystical are by nature unitive and integrative. By implication, any theology of religion that relies exceedingly on dialectics, strong contrasts and disjunctions (the logic of either . . . or) and polarization will in reality be counterproductive, mystically deficient and void of redeeming experience and knowledge. 'If God's love has been poured into our hearts through the Holy Spirit . . .' (Rom. 5.5), this experience of the self-gift of God as life and grace, and contemplation of it within, as well as outside in the historical arena of engagement (though both of these are inextricably intertwined) will open up fresh theological processes attuned to the encounter of religions in the new century. We may recall here that Karl Rahner, picturing the future, once noted: 'The devout Christian of the future will either be a "mystic", one who has "experienced" something, or he will cease to be anything at all.'[6] Nowhere do we realize the truth of such a statement better than when Christians and Christian communities are poised for a fresh encounter with the religious world of their neighbours at the dawn of a new century.

All that I have said evidently also calls for a shift of focus in language. Narratives, images and symbols have a richness and unitive capacity, and in this sense they carry a strong mystical potential. For those who tend to identify the pinnacle of truth with the highest abstraction of meta-discourse, it is possible that images and symbols appear as primitive stages of the mental process with a pale reflection of truth. But in fact, as experience bears out, they are the ways of a much more complete and integral approach to truth. And this is precisely the type of language that we will require in future for our meeting with the religious experience of our neighbours. It will be a language on a different wavelength, and it may not be possible to capture and package it within the prevailing theologies of religion.

Conclusion

It is important to acknowledge that an authentic encounter with the neighbours of other faiths in the new century will not happen unless there is an effort towards a new way of being Christian and preparations for it. This involves being schooled in the universality of the gospel and guided by its spirit of tolerance and peace. Further, meeting with peoples of other faiths will not depend primarily on our having arrived at conclusive explanations and felicitous theological formulae. In any case, much of the present debate will in all likelihood end up inconclusively, impressive though it may appear. The theology of religions which I envisage for the new century is not something from which I expect the most satisfying explanations by virtue of the strength of its dialectics, but one that will be mystical in nature, facilitate a fresh experience of universality, and promote an authentic culture of evangelical tolerance and peace.

Notes

1. Lest there be false expectations, it should be made clear here that the purpose of this article is very limited, and it does not pretend to present the welter of competing theories in the theology of religions, nor to discuss the doctrinal issues connected with them.

2. For the defence of traditional positions, cf. Sybille Toennies, *Der Westliche Universalismus. Eine Verteidigung klassischer Positionen,* Opladen [2]1997.

3. I am reminded of the policeman Javert in Victor Hugo's *Les Miserables.* In Javert's frame of mind, the whole world is an unambiguously chartered territory of black and white.

4. Cf. Zygmunt Bauman, *Moderne und Ambivalenz. Das Ende der Eindeutigkeit,* Frankfurt 1996.

5. Cf. *Asian Christian Perspectives on Harmony. A Document of the Theological Advisory Commission of the Federation of Asian Bishops' Conferences,* FABC Paper No. 75, Hong Kong 1996.

6. Karl Rahner, *Theological Investigations* 7, London 1971, 15.

Images of God and Human Images: The Paradigm of Sexuality

Regina Amnicht Quinn

1. The world today

The world at the end of this century is characterized by a collapse of biographical structures. What previous generations understood as destiny and were able to bear now seem to us to be moral questions: questions about our actions. Normal biography has become selective biography,[1] and the times when one can count on constant structures in life are getting shorter and shorter.

The structures of relationships are directly affected by this change. Thus marriage, which is no longer based on a common 'cause' but on the presence of a particular feeling, is itself becoming fragile in the midst of the disintegrating structures of life. At the same time it is being re-romanticized as a counter-world, as a place which is not the market, where there is no stress: a place of meaning and wholeness.[2] In the gulf which opens up between the real failure and the exaggerated ideal a large number of new forms of organizing our social life are becoming established, which are also forms of organization for sexual life. The most significant of these seems to be so-called 'serial monogamy', in which men and women enter into a series of new sexual partnerships once the old partnership seems to have lost its inner justification, since feeling has disappeared.

'Serial monogamy' as a form of organization is itself by no means an extreme marginal phenomenon, but a central phenomenon. It is sandwiched between, on the one hand the claim made not only by the church but also by the middle-class world that sexuality should be exclusively related to marriage and that marriage should be permanent, and on the other a sexualized public which has borrowed a slogan from the cigarette industry and applied it to sexuality: 'Enjoyment without regret'.

II. A doubly critical view

The language of theological ethics is not only legitimate but indispensable, both in this situation and about this situation. However, this language has become difficult, since it must address this current situation and at the same time maintain an analytical detachment from it. In the face of the collapse of social order the question 'What is right? What should I do?', which presupposes a fixed order, a life running along fixed tracks, becomes the question 'How should I be? What can I do'. This reformulation of the question is focussed less on the achievement of a moral optimum than on the possibility of becoming a moral person.[3] As a result of this, the language of theological ethics about sexuality necessarily changes: it becomes at the same time more modest and more demanding. It becomes more modest, because it withdraws the claim to set out a complex and complete system of rules by the acceptance and observation of which people's lives become 'correct'; and it becomes more demanding by taking as its theme the fundamental enabling of moral identity: it poses itself the task of bringing out and maintaining, time and again, the connection between moral identity and sexual identity.

So what is needed is an approach which is critical in two directions: critical of one's own – Christian – history and critical of one's own – secular – present.

In this doubly critical approach, the language of theological ethics about sexuality becomes a model for theological talk generally at the end of our century. Its fundamental concern is to make a critical examination of its own history and the history of its influence and of the connection between that and people's own self-understanding and roots. The important thing is for theological language to develop as self-referential language, making possible an understanding of current cultures in which they can be heard and understood.

III. Sexuality and Christian self-understanding.

For sexuality, that means that the lack of sayings of Jesus about individual sexual practices and forms of sexual life which are in question today must not be overplayed in a fundamentalistic way. Instead, two attitudes of Jesus which appear in the Gospels could become important. The first is Jesus' attitude to human *corporeality*, which becomes evident in his healings: in particular the restoration of bodily health and wholeness becomes a sign of the dawn of the kingdom of God.[4] The second is Jesus' attitude towards the *commandments relating to cleanness* in his time:[5] with his shifting of the problem of cleanness from the body to the human heart, evaluations also shift. Then it is a desire to harm, a lack of respect, a lack of concern, a lack of love that becomes unclean, rather than the efflux of human sperm or contact with a woman.

Such a brief reference to the biblical evidence cannot be used to demonstrate that Christianity gave Eros poison to drink, as Nietzsche put it very much later, a poison from which Eros may not have died, though it did degenerate into a vice.[6] Nevertheless the history of Christianity has followed a course on which it becomes difficult to contradict Nietzsche. For three factors were essential in the establishment of the early church. Existential attitudes which derived their significance from the high tension of the 'last days' became laws as a result of the failure of the parousia to materialize. The spirit of the time came to influence the early church: the Roman law and Roman medicine of the first Christian centuries and Graeco-Roman high popular philosophy were all united in the way in which they distanced themselves from the body and devalued sexuality on hygienic or moral grounds. Finally, from the end of the third century, the fall was interpreted as a sexual event or an event connected with sexuality.

These three factors developed into a Christian mainstream for which an anthropological dualism and the scepticism about the body and hostility towards the body associated with it made a relaxed and friendly attitude towards sexuality impossible. Instead of such an attitude, tragedies developed time and again. In these tragedies God takes the side of a bourgeois mentality which is hostile to sexuality; the result is a connection between 'God' and 'anxiety', and finally a connection between 'God' and 'death'. This connection, which is diametrically opposed to the Christian understanding of God, yet was produced by it, clearly needs to be broken now, a century later. This poses theology as a whole the task of outlining a picture of God for which freedom and love are not opposites; a picture of God the magnitude of which is not diminished by setting men and women free, but is shown precisely in this liberation.

IV. Consequences

Such an image of God forms the basis of a changed way of talking about sexuality in theological ethics. This change becomes evident above all from three factors.

First of all, it is not enough for moral theology to develop special norms for the sphere of sexuality. This separates sexuality off from life and gives rise to a concept of sexuality which begins from the dangers attached to it, rather than from the possibilities that it offers. The norms and values which govern the whole of life apply in the sphere of sexuality: above all respect for human dignity and the negation of power.

Secondly, it is not enough to talk about sexuality in a one-sidedly discursive language. Moral theology must find a language which does not begin by laying down norms but narrates experiences, which are then linked up with a complex of meaning from which they can be interpreted.

Thirdly, it is not enough for sexuality to be isolated and reduced to the genitalia. The question of sexual identity must be linked up with reflection on the body and corporeality.

This association of sexuality with the human body and human corporeality will then provide possibilities of defining the language of theological ethics about sexuality – not only structurally, but also in terms of content. Then criteria for the development of sexuality can be outlined by which the connection between sexual and moral identity becomes clear.

The first criterion is that of *a clearly contoured corporeality*. This task of giving clear contours and form to the limits of one's own body has different levels in the relationship of men and women to themselves and to the world. Clearly contoured limits to the body mean that one human being can be grasped by the other as a person who does not become arbitrarily evasive and change role, remaining not only unassailable but also intangible. Furthermore, clearly contoured limits to the body can be drawn only when one's own bodily nature is lived out. Love of self, without which love of others becomes impossible, is here made subordinate and stabilized through respect for and in one's own corporeality, without which respect for the corporeality of others becomes empty. It is the perception and shaping of the limits of one's own body, and respect for these limits, that first offers the possibility of recognizing a situation stamped by violence and abuse and of protecting others from self-destruction – which can also be disguised as love.

The second criterion is that of *corporeality bound up with history*. Contrary to a narcissistic feeling of timelessness, of life only in the here and now, corporeality is always exposed to time and must be perceived to be historical. The body is the place of human contingency; it is the place where past and future manifest themselves simultaneously. In this way corporeality bound up with history points on the one hand to its anchorage in the sequence of generations, and on the other to the relationship of all action to the future. From this perspective, sexual activity in particular becomes activity in which past and future are present, and into which responsibility for the future must be incorporated.

The third criterion is that of *corporeality constituted in solidarity*. The philosopher Zygmunt Bauman observes that the motto of the French Revolution, 'Freedom, Equality, Brotherhood', has changed; it now shapes culture as the motto 'Freedom, Difference, Tolerance'.[7] But mere tolerance is not enough. For while tolerance marks the end of wars (of faith), it is at the same time a factor of indifference and distancing. Tolerance must be turned into solidarity. 'A common destiny would also get by with reciprocal tolerance; a divided destiny calls for solidarity.'[8] Only from the perspective of solidarity does responsibility for oneself and others become a single, indivisible attitude.[9]

If in this way corporeality is constituted as solidarity; if responsibility for myself and for others becomes the same attitude, that has consequences for sexuality. Sexuality cannot then be utilized either as a commodity or as a means of power. It is not a commodity for sale within the capitalist system of surplus value, a commodity which can be sold or exchanged; it cannot even be exchanged for affection, tenderness, attention or love. Here sexuality becomes false coinage. Sexuality is not a means of power, nor can it be compelled by power. Its worst perversion is the sexual exploitation and oppression of dependents – whether at home in the family or abroad as sex tourism. Sexuality is not a commodity but a gift; sexuality is not a means of power but a power. Corporeality constituted in solidarity thus ties sexuality to the person and persons; in this way it embodies the necessary resistance against the two great dangers to which sexual activity is exposed: alienation and violence.

These three criteria of a clearly contoured corporeality, a corporeality bound up with history, and a corporeality constituted in solidarity do not offer a fixed system of rules which covers every problem, actual and potential, and its solution. Rather, they are cornerstones and markers: sexuality can be lived out by them, since they hold open the prospect that the connection between sexuality and life is a meaningful one.

Today we face the task of avoiding tragedy for our children and preventing them from being torn apart by a split – whether this is the 'old' split between moral order and their own wishes and needs, or the 'new' split of a sexualized environment and their own anxieties and uncertainties.

V. Gains and losses

The changed structures in the world in which we live and the changes in sexuality bring both gains and losses. The greatest loss is the loss of order, which in the case of sexuality shows itself as a loss of moral rules and thus as the collapse of certainties by which sexual life can be lived 'rightly'. However, the physical uncertainty which arises from this also provides an opportunity: the 'old' task of adapting a sexual identity as seamlessly as possible gives way to the new task of developing one's own identity as sexual identity also. This new task tends to ask too much of people, but at the same time it is a step towards a fundamental new authenticity of sexual identity.

The second loss is that of a particular image of sexuality – sexuality as a mysterious power which commands respect. We are eye-witnesses to the demystification of sexuality and the establishment of sexuality as part of everyday life. The most blatant contrast to the aura of mystery which was part of sexuality is the fact that the semantics of sexual discourse has often become assimilated to the semantics of sports. Sexuality is then associated with physical activity and youth, with achievement, training and a fair treatment of one's partner.[10] This demystification of sexuality is commercialized and remystified in the name of being young, beautiful and fit.

However, neither demystification or remystification can embrace sexuality as a total phenomenon: a remnant remains which is our ultimate concern. This experience offers an opportunity: sexuality in an age in which ordinances are collapsing could establish itself in demystified or remystified form, but only as a mystery. In the concept of mystery we can again trace in sexuality something of that which lies beyond everyday life, something of its overwhelming power which in the last resort cannot be domesticated. Sexuality as a mystery calls not only for enlightenment and practice, but also for awe, fascination and reverence. Sexuality is a mystery which at the same time calls for and needs critical faculties if it is not to lose the immediacy and openness which marks it out as a linguistic phenomenon – one that can be talked about.

When the word which people speak to one another becomes flesh, when the limits of the body are transcended and at the same time re-established, the nearness of religious experience to sexual experience emerges. Both experiences are often endangered and can be perverted; nevertheless both experiences have a part in a fundamental formulation of being man and being woman as transcendent categories.

Translated by John Bowden

Notes

1. Cf. Ulrich Beck and Elisabeth Beck-Gernshei, *Das ganz normale Chaos der Liebe,* Frankfurt am Main 1990, 13.

2. Cf. ibid., 20ff., 222ff.

3. Cf. Dietmar Mieth, 'Christliche Anthropologie und Ethik der Geschlechter angesichts der Herausforderung gegenwärtiger Erfahrung und zeitgenössischen Denkens', in Theodor Schneider (ed.), *Mann und Frau – Grundproblem theologischer Anthropologie*, Freiburg, Basel and Vienna 1989, 167–99.

4. Cf. e.g. Gerd Theissen, *The Miracle Stories of the Early Christian Tradition*, Edinburgh 1982.

5. E.g. Mark 7.15; Luke 11.43ff. Cf. L. William Countryman, *Dirt, Greed, and Sex. Sexual Ethics in the New Testament and Their Implications for Today*, Philadelphia and London 1990.

6. Cf. Friedrich Nietszche, *Beyond Good and Evil*, IV no.168.

7. Cf. Zygmunt Bauman, *Moderne und Ambivalens. Das Ende der Eindeutigkeit*, Frankfurt am Main 1995, 128.

8. Ibid., 287.

9. Ibid.

10. Cf. Niklas Luhmann, *Liebe als Passion. Zur Codierung von Intimität*, Frankfurt am Main [4]1984, 203f.

Liberation from the Straits of Church Morality

Dietmar Mieth

I. Against Incapacitation – Towards an open Catholicity – The Cologne Declaration of 6 January 1989

Ten years ago the Cologne Declaration, the spirit of which was endorsed by 700 theologians from all over the world, saw 'signs of a change in the post-conciliar church'. These were signs:

– of a creeping structural change in the over-extension of the hierarchy of jurisdiction;
– of a progressive incapacitation of the particular churches, a refusal to engage in theological argument and a neglect of the laity in the church;
– of an antagonism from above which accentuates the conflicts in the church by imposing discipline.

In response the Cologne Declaration, among other things, formulated the following statements:

– Not all the teachings of the church are equally sure theologically and of equal importance. We oppose the violation of this doctrine of the degrees of theological certainty or of the 'hierarchy of truths' in the practice of granting or refusing the church's permission to teach. So individual and detailed questions of ethics and dogma cannot arbitrarily be inflated so that they become a question of the identity of faith, while moral attitudes directly connected with the practice of faith (for example opposition to torture, racial segregation or explanation) do not seem to be of the same theological importance for the question of the truth.

The Cologne Declaration was directed in particular against addresses by the pope to theologians and bishops in which 'without taking any account of the degree of certainty and the differing weight of church statements he links teaching about birth control to fundamental truths of faith like the holiness of God and redemption through Jesus Christ in such a way that critics of the papal doctrine about birth control find themselves confronted with "attacking fundamental pillars of the Christian faith", and indeed, when they appeal to the dignity of the conscience, of incurring the error of making the "cross of Christ in vain", destroying the "mystery of God" and denying "human dignity". The concepts of "fundamental truth" and "divine revelation" are being used by the pope to put forward a highly specialized doctrine which cannot be grounded either in holy scripture or in the tradition of the church' (cf. the addresses of 15 October and 12 November 1988).

The most recent declaration by the Papal Advisory Council on the Family of July 1998 takes up seamlessly such attempts to present as 'definitive' teaching which was announced in 1968 as 'not infallible'.

II. 1998: the increase of church control

The year 1998 saw another increase in the number of domesticating texts from the Vatican, most recently including the compulsory consensus of bishops' conferences or the right of Rome to intervene if even just one bishop appeals in deviation. Earlier, objections to lay preaching; to counselling in cases of conflict in pregnancies in Germany; to parts of the ecumenical consensus on the doctrine of justification; and to a differentiated interpretation of the church's claims to truth, had been matters of concern. Here an increase in the number of authoritarian texts is always also a sign of the anxiety of a ruling system that its influence is on the decline. If the charism of authority declines, the bureaucracy has the say, but the inelastic Roman apparatus has long since ceased to be able to cope with the plurality of regional creativity and the diversity of reception. Nevertheless, the ever more powerful blows from Rome cause suffering and misery for the committed members of local churches. Already one cannot fail to perceive the disappointment, anxiety, sorrow and anger shown by people who are ultimately responsible for the local churches and are concerned that decay should not sap the vigour of church life. Rome's demands on the quality, the psychological stability and the resilience of church workers are steadily increasing. One can only hope that the senior pastors of the church are sleeping better than those whose souls they are wounding.

The appearance of this issue of *Concilium* ten years after the Cologne Declaration is an occasion once again, at least by way of a supplement, to recall the fatal situation in which the church not only finds itself but into which its leadership has brought it, and to recall a few Catholic truths in connection with this:

1. The pope is not the bishop of bishops. The regulation of the teaching and pastoral offices by Rome obscures the communicative apostolicity of the Catholic Church. The task of the Petrine service in strengthening sisters and brothers in faith must not lead to a weakening of their credibility locally.

2. It is no longer clear what must definitively be held to be true if Rome claims for itself the sole right to define what is logically or historically so bound up with revelation that in order to safeguard the principles of faith it must be regarded as true. Moreover a circular argument develops when people in the church are forced by church law to believe some things 'definitively', with the intention of later pronouncing what has been achieved by discipline definitively and infallibly as the unanimous consent of the church. This kind of domination cannot be backed up by truths from the tradition. Nor is it possible any longer to accept the Roman fanaticism for certainty. Teachers of theology in priestly seminaries in the Third World – and presumably also many of the theologians of the northern hemisphere who are no longer accustomed to scholastic theology – can often no longer understand the party jargon in which Rome compels them to swear oaths or by which they are measured. They only understand it to mean that they may not contradict and that any deviation will be punished. On the other hand, bishops who have enough to do in coping with poverty and misery put the Roman papers on one side without reading them. They have other concerns.

3. Those who attempt to filter something positive from the message of disciplining the faith by church law must as theologians introduce so many qualifications that they are no longer understood even by well-trained theological colleagues. The messages from Rome about the laity and women; the supervision of theologies and regional churches, which is necessarily limited by a small Roman apparatus to a few questions which often seem peripheral; the Roman pedantries in ecumenical dialogue and the general legalistic mentality disseminated by the Vatican (e.g. in the long controversy over the remarriage of divorced persons or the celibacy of priests), confirm the prejudices cherished by a society which in any case is critical of institutions, and at the same time burden or dishearten the committed members of the church in their task of handing down the faith. The constantly shortened Roman reins, which have so little to do with pastoral practice, do not produce the 'sense of fellowship' that they

claim to strive for. This feeling emerges, rather, at lively and variegated popular church gatherings or Catholic conferences. There it also becomes clear – and we may be grateful for this – that the messages about demarcation are not arriving.

4. On the great changes that are developing in science, technology or the economy Rome speaks either in too abstract a way or not at all. One would like to understand this restraint as an encouragement for the laity to come of age, were it not that on the other side any suspected speck of dust would be blown away by the educated white Western part of the church, e.g. in objections to counselling in conflict in pregnancy within that part of the German legislation which here most reflects questionable morality, namely compulsory counselling. Here too those who are bearing witness locally to a Christian practice which is being lived out are being disheartened (see below).

5. Those in the church who in the face of anger, mourning and a retreat into a private eclectic Christianity show courage and confidence and are ready to state their commitment must often feel misused. For in being relieved of the burden, at the same time they reinforce the system of domination. By looking forward they assuage the fury. In this role, in which their own spontaneous insights and feelings must constantly be repressed, people feel constantly violated.

6. Theologians who make critical statements have difficulties when they are insecure in church institutes and inconveniences when they are secure in the academic sphere. With its interventions in academic careers, Rome is exploiting the academic system and the career paths which are dependent on its approval against these theologians. Why German theology, which is well represented among the German bishops, has referred all life-time first appointments to professorial chairs to Rome is incomprehensible. There is not need to follow Rome's every wish. In Europe, by no means all bishops refer first appointments to Rome. Unfortunately the climate of a hierarchical double supervision in the countries of Central Europe is not only failing to produce a new generation of perceptibly more assimilated scholars, but is also thwarting a large number of theologians, who mumble into their beards (they are in fact almost exclusively men) and weep on each others' shoulders, instead of making clear statements on the basis of their competence, as public academic figures. By this approach, critical spokesmen can easily be isolated psychologically. Here there must be a resolute call in theology for more courage and solidarity.

7. Everyone knows that not all the problems of the church are of its own making. But given the problems which in any case dog accounts of faith and testimonies of faith in the modern world, we could well do without home-made problems in the church. One example of this is the German discussion on the involvement of church institutions in compulsory counselling.

III. A discussion of the problems raised by counselling on conflicts in pregnancy by the letter from the pope to the German bishops dated 11 January 1998

Counselling in a conflict in pregnancy is by German law (§§ 218/219) a legal obligation for any woman who is grappling with the possibility of an abortion in the first three months.

In his letter, the pope expresses fears about 'ambiguities' caused by the involvement of church advisory bodies in legal counselling over conflicts in pregnancy. Here he is concerned that the church position should be clearly defined. Therefore he requests the bishops 'to redefine the church's activity in counselling, to ensure that the freedom of the church is not infringed and that church institutions cannot be made jointly responsible for killing innocent children'. Here he has the 'doctrinal implications' of the pastoral questions in mind, but at the same time he sees compulsory counselling as having 'a key function in carrying out abortions with impunity'. However, compulsory counselling is the strongest restriction on the option for abortion in German law.

In my view it is the pope's statement about an existing ambiguity which produces the situation on which it reports. According to the words of the pope, one can always appeal to him for such a situation. Previously this analysis existed only in isolation in the German Conference of Bishops and not at all in the advisory centres or among the church public or the secular public.

Certainly the situation of a few outsiders has wrongly been denounced here, but only through the pope's letter did this denunciation have the effect that it formerly failed to have.

The problems raised here are by no means small ones. The reason for the clear stance of the bishops in establishing counselling for life with the help of the legally prescribed social measure of compulsory counselling (and the money allocated to it) was that the so-called 'counselling ticket' is not the basis for the legitimation of an abortion, but rather the woman's decision in an emergency. The link between the woman's decision and the counselling lies at the level of the social measures which, along with the social laws (for mother and child), are meant to facilitate the carrying through of pregnancies. Consequently compulsory counselling is attacked not only by Rome but also, for quite different reasons, by spokespersons for the right of abortion.

Those who cast doubts on the involvement of the church in compulsory counselling not only produce the twilight situation referred to above, but also attack the plurality of authorities engaged in compulsory counselling. They become exposed to the charge of failing to perceive an occasion for protecting life, the very charge which the papal letter regards as intolerable. The 'doctrinal implications' must not lead to a refusal of help in the name of an uncompromising symbolic stand. That could not appeal to Jesus of Nazareth, who in cases of doubt decided for fellowship with the sinners rather than with the hypocrites.

Furthermore, in moral theological terms, no danger to the church's teaching can be recognized. So-called *cooperatio formalis*, complicity, does not arise, since the issue is not one of a permit for abortion and since, as the papal letter also concedes, the context is one of legal impunity, not legality. To insist on punishment is not the only way of protecting life effectively; indeed, the efficacy of stricter penal laws is more than disputed.

In the church, too, the condemnation of an action cannot be recognized from the sentence. How else could we understand the fact that while church law lays down excommunication for the killing of unborn life, it punishes abduction, rape and murder with mild church penalties (cf. Canon 1937 with Canon 1336 and Canon 1398)? The 'ambiguity' which thus arises is a real scandal, both doctrinally and pastorally.

Moral theology certainly sees very serious moral implications in the existing German law on conflicts in pregnancy and abortion, despite a recognition of the difference between law and morality, for example in the late abortion of already viable children on genetic grounds, in the tendency of legislation to make legal impunity the basis of the legitimation of the avoidance of 'wrongful life', and in the failure to realize the need for social law to make possible the affirmation of life that is coming to be. If a papal statement were to draw attention to this, that would be an important objection. But in the case of compulsory counselling one can only call on the church authorities to investigate whether an ambiguity in church action does not first arise when persons or institutions authorized by the church cease to participate in compulsory counselling for women in the context.

IV. Liberation from the straits of church morality

Liberation from these straits is possible only when the church ceases to intensify its morality selectively, especially in the spheres of sexuality, family ethics and the protection of unborn life. The very selection of issues for attention heightens the intensity and thus makes a link between the ethos of Christian faith and individual and relational morality. As a result, Christian social ethics loses sharpness on the institutional side and also the foresight and power to grapple with new, future worlds. The church is fortifying islands which are easily circumnavigated by progress. The Polish science-fiction author Stanislaw Lem has put it like this:

> From time to time the church can battle with progress, but if it defends one front, shall we say the inviolability of conception, progress, instead of engaging in a frontal battle, engages in an encircling manoeuvre with which it liquidates the significance of the positions being defended.

Lem enlarges on this insight, formulated from the perspective of the third millennium, with the comment:

> A thousand years ago our church defended motherhood, and then science liquidated the concept of the mother by first splitting the office of motherhood into two parts; then transferring it out of the body, i.e. outside; and finally achieving the synthesis of the embryo, so that after three centuries its defence had lost any significance. Afterwards the church had to agree artificial insemination and *in vitro* fertilization, birth in a machine and the spirit in the machine and the machine itself, which took part in the sacrament, and the disappearance of the difference between natural and artificial being.[1]

Indeed, while the church has made statements in the recent past, e.g. between *Casti Connubii* (1931) and *Humanae Vitae* (1968), it has not grappled at all with the technological, ecological and economic future; or if so, only in a very selective and abstract way.

Church morality is so strongly associated with sexuality, family and the protection of unborn life that one gets the impression that it is trying to make people in the church agents of personal guilt by establishing norms for their life of such a kind that once again they can set their hope only on the mediation of grace through the saving institution.

In the face of this, ethical discussion on a social level is a new need; indeed a boom in ethical questions is unmistakable. The church does not profit from this, though moral theologians do, and one must ask oneself why the church as a moral institution can go so far astray that there is a heavy burden on its constructive participation in the moral future. Certainly there are also examples to the contrary, for example the clarity with which there is talk of the priority of the poor and the priority of work in social ethics. However, such options are always bound up with restraint towards structural demands. Here fortunately there is often more critical and constructive power in the particular churches.

But the planning of a future would in the scientific, technological, economic, ecological and cultural spheres often leaves the formally moral objections of the church behind. Here Rome is risking nothing. Here Rome is present only on the periphery. Despite all the concern for academic and scientific dialogue, this is not really functioning. The disciplinary style of the church is not credible in dialogue; it plays a role only in exploring political effects. In morality, the spiritual leadership is stuck in the straits. Here liberation is necessary, with more courage for clarity, albeit bound up with an awareness of provisionality and the risk of reversals.

Translated by John Bowden

Notes

1. Stanislaw Lem, *Sterntagebücher*, Frankfurt 1978, 250.

Bibliography

Judith A. Dwyer (ed.), *Questions of Special Urgency. The Church in the Modern World. Two Decades after Vatican II?*, Georgetown 1986; see especially Richard McCormick, '"*Gaudium et Spes*"' and the Bioethical Signs of the Times', 79–98.

Hans Küng and Leonard Swidler (eds), *The Church in Anguish. Has the Vatican betrayed Vatican II?*, San Francisco 1987

Dietmar Mieth, 'Tradierungsprobleme christlicher Ethik. Zur Motivationsanalyse der Distanz von Glaube und Kirche', in Erich Feifel and Walter Kasper (eds), *Tradierungskrise des Glaubens*, Munich 1987, 101–38 *Glaubensbekenntnis und Treueid. Klarstellungen zu den 'neuen' römischen Formeln für kirchliche Amsträger. Mit Beiträgen von Gustave Thils und Theodor Schneider*, Mainz 1990

Peter Hünermann and Dietmar Mieth (eds), *Streitgespräch um Theologie und Lehramt. Die Instruktion über die kirchliche Berufung des Theologen in der Diskussion*, Frankfurt am Main 1991

Dietmar Mieth (ed), *Moraltheologie im Abseits? Antwort auf die Enzyklika 'Veritatis Splendor'*, Quaestiones disputatae 153, Freiburg, Basel and Vienna 1994

Adrian Holderegger (ed.), *Fundamente der Theologischen Ethik. Bilanz und Neuansätze*, Studien zur Theologischen Ethik 72, Fribourg 1996

The 'Definitive' Discourse of the Magisterium: Why be Afraid of a Creative Reception?

Christoph Theobald

Clearly 'truths stated definitively' have multiplied over these past years. The recent teaching that priestly ordination is exclusively reserved for males immediately comes to mind, but other examples from the moral sphere remain in our collective memory, like the teaching of the encyclical *Humanae vitae* (1968) on certain acts of contraception which are 'intrinsically evil' with regard to the natural law. However, a more refined historical analysis will show that since the nineteenth century the pontifical magisterium has issued numerous statements of the same kind: the condemnation of religious freedom in the *Syllabus*, judgments on facts in the Bible, authors, facts considered historical, and so on. These have always been linked to specific cultural situations or a state of research, but have then fallen into disuse before sometimes being discreetly corrected. Who for example still defends the thesis of monogenism to safeguard the dogma of original sin? But in 1950 this was the position of the encyclical *Humani generis*, and there was no appeal against it.

So in a sense we are facing an ongoing practice. However, recently there has been a shift in the rules of the game relating to this practice, the subtle architecture of the magisterial authorities and the way in which what it presents to the faithful to believe and to hold is described. One can even ask what the priority now is. Is it a particular problem that has to be resolved – contraception, ordination reserved exclusively for males, etc. – and the discernment of the pontifical magisterium on it? Or is it the establishment of a new regulatory system to indicate the obedience due to the official response? If the centre of gravity of the Roman interventions is in fact shifting increasingly from their content to the formal relations between those who hold authority and those who must obey it, must we not see at work here a subtle strategy of immunization aimed at preventing the debate from continuing and disturbing the Christian people, not to mention a way of hiding the weakness of a particular argument? Clearly one would need to examine, case by case, these doctrines proposed 'definitively' and evaluate their arguments in order to confirm or disconfirm what is only a suspicion. However, that is not the object of this article. I want, rather, to reflect on the significance of the actual establishment of a new rule of the game, published for the first time in 1989 and recently introduced in the 1983 Code of Canon Law.[1] Why this change, and what diagnosis of the historical situation of the church by its supreme authorities does it represent?

Three 'baskets' of Catholic truths

First of all, let us recall briefly the essential elements in doctrines and questions, the subtlety of which probably escapes the vast majority of Christians. They are in fact addressed to those who exercise a teaching function in the church, to the bishops but also and above all to the theologians, asking them to make a profession of faith before taking up their posts or on certain other occasions (as at the beginning of an ecumenical council).

Since antiquity, the common faith which binds the faithful together and gathers them in communities or churches in communion among themselves and with Peter's successor has been set out in creeds, especially the Niceno-Constantinopolitan creed, the rule of interpreting the Scriptures and tradition, which also includes the new profession of faith (1989). The creed in a way precedes the opening of three 'baskets', in which all the truths to be believed and held are, or could be, arranged. In the first basket – according to the Latin tradition, this is broader than the simple creed – is the whole content of faith, though the documents do not indicate what this is, being simply content to describe the authorities which determine it or the way in which it is 'arranged': 'all the truths which are contained in the Word of God written or handed down by the tradition *and* put forward by the church to be believed as having been divinely revealed, whether by virtue of a solemn judgment (conciliar or pontifical) or by the ordinary and universal Magisterium', according to the famous distinction of Vatican I,[2] to which we shall return. We should already keep in mind that it indicates an unfathomable depth in the Word of God received by the tradition, a depth which the defined statements, dogmas deposited on the surface of the awareness of the church, risk hiding. Cardinal Ratzinger's 1998 commentary gives some examples of these dogmatic truths: in addition to the articles of the Creed they are the various christological and Marian dogmas, the doctrine of the institution of the sacraments by Christ and their efficacy in conferring grace, etc.[3]

Then comes a second basket in which are laid out doctrines relating to faith and morals, the specific character of which is that they are 'necessary for keeping and presenting faithfully the deposit of faith'. This is precisely the place where the examples of 'truths put forward definitively', mentioned at the beginning of this article, belong. Furthermore, the commentator from the Congregation for the Doctrine of Faith enumerates them himself,[4] adding that 'their definitive character is implied by their intrinsic connection with revealed truth'.[5] Here he puts his finger on the key point of the system of regulation, the frontier at which revelation touches the history of cultures, with its series of new questions that have haunted the Christian conscience since the beginning of modern times. Is revelation definitively bound by a pre-modern vision of the historicity of the biblical narratives and what they say about the origins, by the fact that Jesus is not said to have conferred apostolic identity on women, etc.?[6] Must it obey an interpretation of natural law which has hardly been touched, if at all, by the achievements of the human sciences?

If the new profession of faith exempts certain facts bound up with the deposit of faith from historical fluctuations and the meanderings of the public debate between theologians, it is because it presupposes, despite superficial distinctions, that there is a profound link between 'baskets' of truths. The official commentary even suggests 'communicating vessels', since the authorities which regulate the flow from one to another are strictly the same as those which determine the content of the first basket: what constitutes the most common ecclesial awareness of revelation, represented by the ordinary and universal magisterium, can be confirmed or reaffirmed at the moment of a challenge – thus the commentary – as definitive by the Roman Pontiff (second basket), before possibly going into the first basket, where it figures among the defined truths of the deposit of faith. This is a trajectory which was followed, according to the commentary, by the doctrine of papal infallibility and which will be followed – perhaps – by the doctrine that priestly ordination is exclusively reserved to males.[7]

Finally, the third basket, which is furthest from the centre of revelation, contains all the teachings of the bishops and the pope which, without being proclaimed by a definitive act, require of the believer what the text calls 'religious submission of the will and the intellect'. The dimensions of this last receptacle are thus immense; however, the texts do not give any example of the content, perhaps because their interest lies elsewhere.

What is new?

To put it brutally: the *Professio fidei* of 1989, recently introduced into the Code of Canon Law, reproduces the broad outline of the *De magisterio* of the preparatory scheme on the church (1962), a text that was rejected not only by the Central Commission but also by the Council itself.[8] Points deliberately left open by Vatican I and Vatican II for further debate are thus decided with reference to a neo-scholastic conception which is little, if at all, affected by the challenge of history or the current plurality of cultures. Already at the time of the last Council, the conflict related to the following three points:

1. In the face of an intellectualistic conception which regards revelation as the totality of truths to be believed (the instruction model), the majority of fathers emphasized – in line with John XXIII – the internal unity of the Christian mystery (the communication model). Do not the latest texts of the magisterium again hide this insight that was gained, namely that faith comes from listening to the gospel, which is not primarily passive acceptance of a series of doctrines (even if the regulative aspect – the *regula fidei* – is not in any way excluded)[9] but a definitive encounter with Jesus Christ, interwoven with events and words closely bound together, as a place of God's ultimate communication of himself (cf. *Dei Verbum* 2 and 4)? To criticize the intellectualism of the *Professio fidei* is not to fall into a kerygmatic reduction, but to note with the last Council that a cancerous proliferation of doctrines ultimately risks totally blocking any access to faith, which, according to tradition, never stops at formulae (in the plural) but desires to enter into the very intimacy of God.

2. That is why *Lumen Gentium* 25 makes the preaching of the gospel the principle duty of bishops – something that these latest texts, which base themselves almost exclusively on this passage, pass over in silence – before calling them 'authentic teachers . . . endowed with the authority of Christ, who preach the faith to the people assigned to them, the faith which is destined to inform their thinking and direct their conduct'. This duty, not only to preach but also to interpret the gospel with authority in one situation or another, has in fact been fulfilled every day throughout the world since the beginning of Christianity in many ways: this is what Vatican I and Vatican II designate by the technical term 'ordinary and universal magisterium', distinguishing the continuous exercise of it from those few 'extraordinary' occasions when the church adopts a position on

the meaning of the gospel, solemnly and always in opposition to a challenge.

But what is the aim of this distinction? First of all to keep open the infinite depth and breadth . . . of the practice of faith, that of the pastors who proclaim it and that of faithful who live it out, together forming the *sensus fidei* of the people of God' (Lumen Gentium 12). This can never be reduced to any formula, dogma or sacramental rite.[10] Those who today would like to rely on this secular magisterium to resolve the problems they have in interpreting the gospel in a particular cultural context soon discover that they can only circumscribe its authority after the event and at the cost of intensive historical and theological research, simply by reason of its great 'dispersion' in space and time. But the simple fact that such a doctrine is held or such a practice is accepted by all, everywhere and always – *as self-evident* – is not yet a guarantee of truth. So there is a need to discover what, within history, comes from God and is still binding on us, and to distinguish it carefully from what derives from changing historical and cultural circumstances. This evaluation is at the same time the only way of establishing whether a problem that arises is truly new, so that we must resolve it at our own risk and peril. Can one deduce, for example, from the historical fact that neither Jesus nor the apostles nor any witness of the tradition is said to have admitted women to 'apostolic' identity that it is a 'property of the church, infallibly handed down by its ordinary and universal magisterium', and thus definitively binding on us? Only if one can *prove* that they in fact asked themselves the questions that we ask ourselves today: and that is certainly not the case.

To speak immediately here in 'definitive' terms thus risks short-circuiting, even hiding, the complex process in which communities, theologians and the magisterium engage. This consists in listening both to the conscience of the church – the *sensus fidei* – today and to that of the tradition, in order to establish progressively (in a remarkable *conspiratio*) the exact tenor (old or new) of the question that needs to be resolved. Now on this tricky problem the *Professio fidei* and its commentary simply take up the *De magisterio* of 1962, which in turn quotes the encyclical *Humani Generis*:

> Most of the time what is taught and urged (by the encyclicals, etc., as documents of the ordinary magisterium of the church) is already part of Catholic doctrine. If the sovereign pontiffs expressly make a judgment on a matter which was hitherto controversial, everyone will understand that this matter, in the thought and will of the sovereign pontiffs, can no longer be considered to be the object of a free discussion between theologians.[11]

Very strong opposition from the majority within the Central Preparatory Commission[12] and during the Council removed this passage
from *Lumen Gentium* 25 and the 1983 Code (canon 750) also ignores it; it
was introduced in 1998 in the form in which we now know it. Certainly
one can always argue from the fact that 'the successor of Peter is only
confirming or reaffirming a doctrine already taught by the ordinary and
universal magisterium – which necessarily includes that of the pope'. But
can one ignore the fact that the 'universal' in the 'ordinary and universal
magisterium' indicates a theological depth and breadth in the historical
conscience of the church which can have remarkable surprises in store,
particularly in a situation of unprecedented historical acceleration and
cultural pluralism? To use a definitive declaration to stop the debate on
what at least has the appearance of being a new question is to accredit *one*
theology of the magisterium which, in the spirit of Catholic integralism,
risks confusing the always surprising mystery of the Catholic faith with
the conceptual transparency of formulae which, because they are
necessarily impoverished, can do more than point to it.

3. The task of interpreting the gospel has become all the more complex
today since modernity has made us more aware of the historical roots of
the gospel and the diversity of the cultures which are waiting to receive it
creatively. So there is no denying the intrinsic link between the 'treasure'
(*depositum*) and the creative 'field' in which it is hidden. How else are we
to conceive of a revelation which is not already inculturated or
contextualized? Beyond doubt this is the element of truth in talk about
the 'connection'.

But once again the *De magisterio* of 1962 casts its shadow on current
debates. It is in fact this text which for the first time defines the
characteristics of a second basket of Catholic truths: in it there can be
'everything which, without being revealed in an explicit or implicit
manner, is nevertheless linked to revealed matters in such a way that it is
necessary, in order to safeguard the deposit of faith, to explain it correctly
and protect it effectively (*ad tuendam*[13])'; this effectively includes 'the
interpretation and the *infallible* declaration of the natural law and
judgment on the objective conformity of all human actions with the
doctrine of the gospel and the divine law. No field of human actions can
be withdrawn, under its ethical and religious aspects, from the authority
of the magisterium instituted by Christ.' The text even includes, in
relation to historical criticism, the 'authentic judgment on the origin and
nature, and above all the doctrinal and moral value, of the sayings and
extraordinary facts presented as having their origin in God (miracles)'.[14]
Now the last two Councils are not only infinitely more discreet about
what this possible specific 'basket' might contain, but above all leave

open the question of the status of the connection, namely the form of its link with revelation and the place that is occupied, or could be occupied, in this link, by historical reason, the just autonomy of which cannot be denied (*Gaudium et Spes* 36). It is as if the fathers had felt the latent risk of a historical monophysitism, whereas the magisterium has received the charism of keeping the ultimate character of the gospel of God discernible in the history of humankind.

So it must be understood that the *Professio fidei* is not concerned with a particular problem, nor does it simply substitute a new profession for an older one;[15] it truly introduces a new rule of the game – which was already the intention of the redactors of *De magisterio* in 1962. This action is taking place today in a whole series of measures by which, confronted by globalization and cultural pluralism, the magisterium of the Church of Rome is trying to reinforce and to specify in law its transcultural and transhistorical competence in matters of faith, at the same time limiting that of diocesan, national (conferences of bishops) and continental synods, and putting the bar in ecumenical dialogue ever higher. The issue is its conception of the catholicity of faith and the church.[16]

What is at stake with this new regulation?

First of all it can be asked wither such a transformation of the rules of the game by the one who is its guarantor is credible today. Certainly the official commentary on the *Motu proprio* suggests that this is merely an explicitation of 'the faith in the assistance which the Holy Spirit gives to the Magisterium of the Church and the Catholic doctrine of the infallibility of the magisterium'. But what has preceded this allows one to doubt.

The most serious issue is a hermeneutical one. We have in fact become aware of the diversity of cultures, their multiple interactions and the threat that an abstract and systematic globalization poses to all of them. The gospel cannot simply come to them from outside as a transcultural doctrine or a collection of practices and rites, thought to affect them all in their specific corporeality. It has to be received, in order to fall into the ground there before being recreated in some way by those who have already begun to live by it. This infinitely complex process is turning the church of the nations, which is still too structured by Latinism, into a vast laboratory.

Thus to emphasize the birth of faith and the course which each being and each culture should follow does not mean that the way taken by our fathers has no meaning for us, far less that they took the wrong way.

Besides, who would venture to pass judgment on this? But it is certainly important to emphasize today that the necessary recognition of the way taken by others, for example our fathers in the faith,[17] is possible only for those (or more precisely for a particular church) whose faith has already taken, at its risk and peril (i.e. with the assistance of the Holy Spirit), a similar course in own culture. First of all to emphasize the 'irreformable' character of the dogmatic formulations of our tradition (bound up with the cultural context of ancient Europe without being totally subservient to it), or even to urge the objectivity of a complex of doctrines which is definitively to be held, is an approach which threatens to close the way to the recontextualization of faith and finally to prove contrary to the gospel. Certainly the reception of the gospel is always an act of obedience; but this must liberate a real creativity within each culture. And to use the words of the Gospels: would not each culture love to hear Peter say to it one day what Jesus said, 'My daughter, your faith has saved you'?

An unanswered question

But how can one fail to recall here the tremendous, indeed vertiginous, dimensions of such a reconstruction of the Christian tradition, which moreover began some time ago? In fact, during the modern era, at least a part of Christianity has progressively become aware that revelation does not exist outside its historical reception: the paradosis lived out effectively, the body of faith – what it is, what it receives and what it gives itself – is the only trace of its divine origin. So its historical interpretation is part of revelation in the sense that revelation is radically dependent on it.

Understanding itself to be detached from a tradition which would want to give the past or a privileged period of the past an exemplary or untouchable status, Western modernity has in fact resorted to the true eschatological sense of the paradosis, which in the New Testament is based on a great prophetic intuition. As Jeremiah prophesied (31.34): 'Know the Lord, for they shall all know me, from the least of them to the greatest.' Referring to the paradosis, the Christian prophet and apostle are no longer prisoners of a past which must serve as an example, but with their own experience of faith enter into a synchronic relationship with the 'companions of the first hour', to whom they owe everything. That also means that the relationship of immediacy which they maintain with the actuality of revelation authorizes them to interpret creatively at the very level of the witness of the first communities. The withdrawal of the past from its role as a sacred model, which held captive the extraordinary eschatological novelty of faith, is progressively liberating a whole variety of cultural interpretations of the gospel, to the point of 'suspending' its historical effectiveness on the plural capacity of us beings of flesh to receive it by reinterpreting it continually in this or that given context. The post-conciliar debates on the relationship between the uniqueness of Christ and his plural *pneuma* in us are the expression of this on a dogmatic level.

Neither an illusory kerygmatic spiritualization of the paradosis nor a doctrinal fixation on the rule of faith can exorcize the theological vertigo produced by a modernity which delivers over the truth to history and by consequence of our multiple 'ways of doing it' at the same time counts on the internal regulation of the eschatological experience of the holiness of God in our history.[18] How can one fail to see that this prodigious thrust of Christian awareness, apparently provoked from outside but proving to be the result of a mysterious interaction between the church and modern societies, is finally the very fruit of the gospel? That, in my view, is the unanswered question which the recent documents of the magisterium merely indicate in outline.

But who would not readily recognize that this problem is so radical theologically that it can frighten the authorities and prompt them to read out of it what they call a 'spiritual crisis of faith',[19] in the framework of the apocalyptic vision which so stamped official Catholicism between 1870 and 1950, expressing its feeling of living in a state of permanent emergency with the modern world?

In fact this fear is only rarely expressed in public: it is not one that is easy to acknowledge. J. C. Fenton, an expert on the Council and a confidant of Ottaviani, who relates in his diary one of his visits to the cardinal at the end of the first period of the Council, reports having heard one of the cardinal's team explain that 'this time was the time of demons'.[20] In such a situation, to count only on the force of argument would be an illusion. But cannot one hope that the assistance of the Spirit which is so often evoked in the texts of the magisterium is manifesting itself in all, making it possible to conquer fear by faith?

Translated by John Bowden

Notes

1. Cf. Congregation for the Doctrine of Faith, 'Profession of Faith and Oath of Fidelity, 9 January 1989', in *AAS* 81, 1989, 104–16: *Motu proprio Ad tuendam fiden*, in *Osservatore Romano*, 1 July 1998.

2. DH 3011.

3. Doctrinal note 11 (DC 95, 1998, 655).

4. Ibid. Why does the second paragraph of the *Professio fidei* distinguish between *omnia* and *singula* as if the *omnia* did not already contain the *singula*? It is all the more surprising that in the first paragraph 'what is divinely revealed' is simply treated in a global way (*ea omnia quae*).

5. Doctrinal note 6 (DC 95, 1998, 654).

6. The speech by John Paul II to those taking part in a colloquium on the 'roots of anti-Judaism in a Christian milieu' uses the concept of 'supernatural fact' to describe the existence of the Jewish people and the fact that Jesus was a Jew: 'That is why those who consider the fact that Jesus was a Jew and that his milieu was the Jewish world as simply contingent cultural facts, for which it would be possible to substitute another religious tradition from which the person of the Lord could be detached without losing his identity, not only fail to recognize the significance of the history of salvation but more radically strip the incarnation of its truth and make an authentic conception of inculturation impossible' (DC 94, 1997, 1003ff.).

7. Doctrinal note 11 (DC 95, 1998, 655).

8. The conflict in the Central Preparatory Commission began in November 1961 during the debate on a new profession of faith to be used at the opening of the Council and continued in June 1962 in the discussion of *De magisterio*. In both discussions one finds the same opposition ploy and the same arguments; this confirms the link between the texts, which were both rejected.

9. Cf. e.g. Rom. 10.9: 'If you confess with your lips that Jesus is Lord and believe in your heart that God raised him from the dead, you will be saved.'

10. That is also the sense of the negative formulation of the rule of 'unanimous consent' at Trent, Vatican I and Vatican II: 'to accept nothing contrary to that which has always been the sense of the church and its traditions' (cf. DH 1507, 3007 and the regulation of Vatican II, article 40).

11. G. Alberigo and F. Magistretti, *Contitutionis Dogmaticae Lumen Gentium Synopsis Historica,* Istituto per la Scienze Religiose, Bologna 1975, 95–104; cf. also DH 3885.

12. Cf. in particular the intervention by Cardinal Frings in AP II-II, pars IV, 638.

13. This would provide the title for the 1998 *Motu proprio.*

14. *Synopsis* [n.11], 296, 45–58.

15. This was the interpretation of the commentator U. Betti in 1989 (cf. the French edition of *Osservatore Romano*, 7 March 1989, 11).

16. Cf. C. Theobald, 'Le messianisme chrétien. Une manière de s'introduire dans le processus de mondialisation', *RSR* 86/1, 1998, 77–98.

17. Cf. the rule of Vincent of Lerins, *Commonitorium* 2: 'In the Catholic Church itself that must be scrupulously observed which has been believed everywhere, always and by all.'

18. Cf. C. Theobald, 'Les enjeux de la narrativité en théologie', in *Transversalités* (Institut Catholique de Paris) 59, July/September 1996, 43–62.

19. Cf. the article by the secretary of the Congregation of the Doctrine of Faith 'A propos de la réception des Documents du Magistère et du désaccord public', which anticipates the argument of the recent commentary on the *Motu proprio* by Cardinal Ratzinger (*Osservatore Romano*, 20 December 1996 and DC 94, 1997, 111).

20. Extract quoted by G. Ruggieri in G. Alberigo (ed.), *History of the Second Vatican Council*, Vol.2.

Ecclesia Semper Reformanda: Theology as Ideology Critique

Elisabeth Schüssler Fiorenza

> You are the salt of the earth;
> But if salt has lost its taste,
> How shall its saltness be restored?
> (Matt. 5.13)

The most recent attempts of the Vatican to squelch theological discussion reminds one of Dostoievsky's Grand Inquisitor, who must silence Jesus because of his own lack of faith. This politics of silencing rather than dialogue is a far cry from the confidence and vision of Pope John XXIII, who initiated Vatican II in order to call the church to *aggiornamento* – engagement and dialogue. Although the Council spoke of theology only in passing,[1] it nevertheless brought about a profound shift in the function and self-understanding of theology. Theology was to change from its neo-Aristotelian servitude to ecclesiastical interests into a critical dialogical intellectual inquiry. This shift has not just been a theoretical shift but also a shift from theology as the prerogative of the clergy to theology as the task of all the people of G*d.[2]

Since I write as a feminist theologian, and feminist theology begins with critically reflected experience, I want to elaborate this shift with respect to my own experience. On 25 January 1959, when Pope John XXIII announced the Council, I was finishing my first semester of studies. At the time in Germany non-ordinands generally studied theology in combination with other subjects for teaching in public schools, and I had enrolled for theology, German literature and history. On a part-time basis I worked simultaneously in the diocesan youth office. This work included continuing education workshops for priests who would call so-called lay-theology *Schmalspur* [narrow-track] theology. Hence I decided to study the full course of theology which was required of candidates for the priesthood. I was the first wo/man[3] at my university to do so.

However, during the time I was deliberating this decision, rumour had it that Karl Rahner would be silenced. My reaction to this news was to make a solemn promise: if Rahner was silenced I would drop the study of theology, since I was convinced that intellectual integrity and freedom of speech were the *sine qua non* of any theology worth its name. However, if Rahner were not silenced, I would enrol for the full course of theological studies. As we all know, Rahner was not censured, and Pope John XXIII announced the Second Vatican Council. Following the Pope's invitation, the Council sought to open intellectual 'windows and doors' and to engender new theological possibilities and self-understandings. The church on the whole became orientated towards the needs of 'the world' and the future rather than bent on defending its monarchical-patriarchal repressive structures. The study of theology became intellectually exciting and challenging. Karl Rahner emerged as one of the great 'church fathers' of the twentieth century.

In so far as Vatican II elaborated the collegial and familial kinship [brotherhood] dimension of the church, it sought to transform the model of church inherited from the nineteenth century. In accordance with the scriptures, the Council stressed the priesthood of all believers[4] and stated with reference to Gal. 3.28 in *Lumen Gentium* 32:

> By divine institution Holy Church is structured and governed with a wonderful diversity . . . There is in Christ and in the church no inequality on the basis of race or nationality, social condition or sex . . . And if by the will of Christ some are made teachers, dispensers of mysteries, and shepherds on behalf of others, yet all share a true equality with regard to the dignity and activity common to all the faithful for the building up of the Body of Christ . . . For the distinction which the Lord made between sacred ministers and the rest of the people of God entails a unifying purpose, since pastors and the other faithful are bound to each other by a mutual need . . . This very diversity of graces, ministries and works gathers the children of God into one, because 'all these things are the work of one and the same Spirit' (I Cor. 12.11).[5]

This vision of church was an outcome of discursive struggle. In the words of Avery Dulles, *Lumen Gentium* was 'hammered into shape on the anvil of vigorous controversy . . .'[6] The Council proposed its teachings without anathemas and condemnations, orientated the church's mission towards the needs of the world, and emphasized that the church is the pilgrim people of G*d 'made up of sinful men (sic)', in constant need of purification and renewal. At the same time, however, it feels confident of God's loving help which guides its steps . . . because the Church is human, it exists in time and is subject to the forces of history. But because of its divine element, it presses forward full of optimism, toward a goal beyond history. In all its prayer and labour it is sustained by the glorious vision of the final kingdom in which God will be all in all (I Cor. 15.28).[7]

Instead of beginning with the hierarchy and the structures of govern-ance, the Council started with the notion of the church as the people of G*d, asserted that other Christian churches with different institutional structures are 'ecclesial' communities, defined the function of ecclesial office as service rather than domination and authoritarian governance, and redefined church leadership by using the expression 'ecclesiastical ministry' rather than hierarchy. Whereas the Council of Trent taught that ecclesial ministry *consists* of the hierarchy of bishop, priest and deacon, Vatican II teaches that ecclesial ministry is *exercised* in these different orders.[8] However, the Council did not engage in a serious historical and institutional analysis and critique of church structures. The lack of such a critical institutional analysis would prove to be one of the most detrimental legacies and unfinished businesses of the Council. As Ms O'Wedel and other Protestant respondents to the Council documents observed very early on:

> A Protestant misses here a stronger emphasis on a share [of the laity] in the actual government of the church. This may be an area where the Catholic Church will gradually have to make some changes.[9]

The present backlash is impelled by the refusal of the Vatican to make such changes. Catholic churches all round the world have sought to translate the vision of Vatican II into ecclesial praxis. In many parts of the world in the past thirty years the Roman Catholic Church has become a force for social justice, radical democracy and global peace. It has moved from a form of Eurocentric Roman-imperial Catholicism to a pluralistic actualization of world Catholicism that seeks to utilize the gifts and talents of all its people. Yet these developments have not been welcomed and nurtured by the Vatican; rather, they are feared and perceived as spinning 'out of control'. In the past decade or so leading theologians, bishops and sisters have been silenced and have lost their ecclesiastical standing because they acted in the spirit of the Council. The late Penny Lernoux aptly summed up this struggle over the self-understanding of church:

At stake are two different visions of faith: the church of Caesar, powerful and rich, and the church of Christ – loving, poor, and spiritually rich.[10]

The Council interrupted and was believed to have ended for good the regime of silencing and condemnation. The intellectual freedom promised by Vatican II is summed up in the Pastoral Constitution on the Church in the Modern World. After expressing the hope that many of the so-called laity would be schooled in the sacred sciences, the document insists:

In order that such persons may fulfil their proper functions, let it be recognized that all the faithful, clerical and lay, possess a lawful freedom of inquiry and of thought, and the freedom to express their minds humbly and courageously about those matters in which they enjoy competence.[11]

This spirit of open inquiry and research praised and advocated by the Council promised that all totalitarian measures, silencing and inquisitions were a matter of the past – or so we thought at the time. Yet almost twenty years later in 1984, when I had to make the decision to move from a professorship at a Roman Catholic university to a Protestant divinity school, a Catholic colleague encouraged me to do so, arguing that in the foreseeable future 'good', that is intellectually creditable and responsible, theology could be done only at non-Catholic institutions. Unfortunately, Rome has proved him right again and again in the past decade.

The Vatican's criteria for 'faithful submission of will and intellect' increasingly centre on the ordination of wo/men and the legitimization of male office only. Although the Council documents are full of androcentric language, women have taken its vision very seriously and have read its texts in a generic way as applying to ourselves. We have consistently maintained that we must be acknowledged as human and ecclesial subjects with equal rights and dignity rather than remain objects of male theology and clerical governance. Yet our call to conversion from ecclesiastical patriarchy is increasingly met with outright rejection.

While we have denounced the structural and personal sin of patriarchal sexism and have claimed our ecclesial gifts and rights, those who advocate restoration of the pre-Vatican II model of church have appealed to the maleness of Christ, to essential gender differences, and to the scriptural texts of subordination in order to legitimate church practices and structures that exclude from sacramental, doctrinal and governing power all wo/men and those men who are associated with wo/men. For the clerical-patriarchal hierarchy not only is exclusive of wo/men in leadership positions but also establishes itself as a 'woman-free' zone through mandatory celibacy.

Today we seem to have come full circle. Under threat of heavy censure and punishment, the latest *Motu proprio Ad Tuendam Fidem* of 30 June 1998 seeks to eliminate the remnants of 'the lawful freedom of inquiry and of thought and the freedom to express it' that still exist in Catholic institutions. Examples given for the authoritative teachings of the magisterium which may not be questioned are the prohibition of euthanasia and prostitution, and especially the exclusion of women from ordination. It is obvious that this most recent papal decree attempts to silence women's claim to full membership in the church once and for all. Hence the language of the document is more Roman imperial than evangelical-conciliar. Its legalistic measures bespeak the fear of Dostoievsky's Grand Inquisitor:

> In order to safeguard the faith of the Catholic Church against errors springing up among certain of Christ's faithful, especially among those who apply themselves as scholars to the study of sacred theology, it has seemed most necessary to Us, whose chief duty is to confirm Our brothers (*sic*) in the faith (cf. Luke 22.32), that certain norms should be added to the texts of the code of canon Law and of the Code of Canons of the Eastern Churches currently in force, by means of which the duty of upholding the truth definitely proposed by the Church's Magisterium may be expressly imposed and canonical sanctions related to this duty also noted.[12]

Those who disagree are to be warned and then punished as heretics or apostates by excommunication or another appropriate and just penalty. The language of penalization and expulsion from the church rejected by the Council is at work again here. Yet in such a time of intellectual silencing and censure it is more than ever necessary that the faithful are enabled critically to recognize the ideological formation of such ecclesiastical discourse. Theology must learn to understand itself as ideology critique if the spirit of Vatican II is not to be lost for ever. As ideology critique, theology is first of all orientated towards the demystification of hegemonic power relations. The attempts of the magisterium to turn back the clock to Vatican I are best understood in terms of an ideological struggle over what constitutes Catholicity: is it submission of will and intellect to ecclesiastical authority or freedom of conscience and speech in the service of the faithful?

With the feminist theorist Michèlle Barrett I understand ideology as referring to a process of mystification or misrepresentation. Ideology is distorted communication rather than false consciousness.

> The retrievable core of meaning of the term ideology is precisely this: discursive and significatory mechanisms that may occlude, legitimate, naturalize or universalize in a variety of different ways but can all be said to mystify.[13]

A fundamental assumption of critical theory holds that every form of social order entails some forms of domination, and that critical emancipatory interests fuel the struggles to change these relations of domination and subordination. Such power relations engender forms of distorted communication that result in self-deception on the parts of agents with respect to their interests, needs and perceptions of social and religious reality.[14] Theologically speaking they are structural sin.

> The notion of ideology must be situated with a theory of language that emphasizes the ways in which meaning is infused with forms of power . . . To study ideology is not to analyse a particular type of discourse but rather to explore . . . the models whereby meaningful expressions serve to sustain a relation of domination.[15]

John B. Thompson has pointed to three major modes or strategies which are involved in the way ideology operates: legitimization, dissimulation and reification (literally: to make into a thing). All three models can be identified in the Vatican's discourses of censure and repression of free discussion. The first strategy is an appeal for legitimacy on traditional grounds, whereas the second conceals relations of domination in ways that are themselves often structurally excluded from thought. According to Jürgen Habermas, ideology thus serves to 'impede making the foundations of society [or, I would add, the church] the object of thought and reflection'.[16] The third form of ideological operation is reification or naturalization, which represents a transitory, culturally, historically and socially engendered state of affairs as if it were permanent, natural, outside of time or directly revealed by G*d. This ideological strategy comes to the fore in the Vatican's questionable theological arguments for wo/men's special nature and its appeals to the will of Jesus. Moreover ideology contributes to the distorted self-understanding of oppressed people who have internalized belief in the legitimacy of their own subordination and innate status as inferior.

Theology as ideology critique does not come from outside but from inside the church. As immanent critique, it points to the discrepancy between the basic Christian values of freedom well-being (salvation) and equality proclaimed by the Vatican II church and the objective relations of domination structuring its institutions. Both models of church, that of submission and subordination characteristic of Roman imperialism and that of the pilgrim people of G*d, are inscribed in scripture and embedded in tradition. In this struggle over the future of the Catholic Church understood either as a discipleship of equals[17] or as the embodiment of a Grand Inquisitor, theology as ideology critique has an important role to play.

Notes

1. For instance, the index of Walter M. Abbott and Joseph Gallagher (eds.), *The Documents of Vatican II. With Notes and Comments by Catholic, Protestant, and Orthodox Authorities*, Chicago 1966, has very few entries under 'theology' or 'sacred sciences', and most of them refer to the education and training of priests.

2. In this way I seek to indicate the brokenness, ambiguity and indeterminacy of human G*d language.

3. I write wo/man in this way in order to reflect on the theoretical ambiguity of the term. Moreover, I use wo/men as inclusive of men and she as inclusive of he. Just as wo/men in an androcentric language system have already to think twice in order to know whether we are meant or not, so I invite men to learn how to think twice and to ask whether they are meant or not when I use the term.

4. See my book *Priester für Gott*, Münster 1972.

5. Abbott and Gallagher, *Documents* (n.1), 58–9.

6. Avery Dulles, 'The Church', in Abbott and Gallagher, *Documents* (n.1), 11.

7. Ibid. 11.

8. *Lumen Gentium* 28: 'Thus the divinely established ecclesiastical ministry is *exercised* on different levels by those who from antiquity have been called bishops, priests and deacons.' See also Hans Küng, *The Church*, London and New York 1968.

9. Abbott and Gallagher, *Documents* (n.1) 524.

10. Penny Lernous, *The People of God. Struggle for World Catholicism*, New York 1990, 1. See especially 283–364 on the 'big money' fuelling the Vatican crackdown and the international Catholic Right.

11. The Pastoral Constitution on the Church in the Modern World, Part II, Chapter II, Abbott and Gallagher, *Documents* (n.1), 270.

12. Apostolic Letter *Ad Tuendam Fidem* given *Motu proprio* by Pope John Paul II, see *Origins* 16 July 1998.

13. Michèlle Barrett, *The Politics of Truth. From Marx to Foucault*, Stanford 1991, 177.

14. Raymond A. Morrow, *Critical Theory and Methodology*, Thousand Oaks 1994, 130–49.

15. John B. Thompson, *Studies in the Theory of Ideology*, Cambridge 1984, 254.

16. Jürgen Habermas, 'Ideology', in Tom Bottomore (ed.), *Modern Interpretations of Marx*, Oxford 1981, 166.

17. See my books *In Memory of Her*, New York and London 1983, and *Discipleship of Equals. A Critical Feminist Ekklesialogy of Liberation*, New York and London 1993.

The Ordination of Women: A Test Case for Conciliarity

Angela Berlis

This issue of *Concilium* is concerned with unanswered questions in theology after the Second Vatican Council. The working title for this article was: 'Women and Ecumenism as Illustrated by the Ordination of Women'. Where is the unanswered question there? Does it lie in the fact that on the one hand an increasing number of churches are ordaining women, not only the churches of the Reformation but also those which explicitly understand themselves as churches of the Catholic tradition, whereas on the other hand very recent official Roman Catholic declarations increasingly state that this course can never be taken? Does it consist in the fact that the ecumenical discussion of this question in the future will increasingly be thrown out of balance: whereas Roman Catholic theologians are obliged to keep out of the discussion and be submissive on questions of the ordination of women as a result of the most recent declarations of the Roman see, other churches no longer see the ordination of women but their non-ordination as a problem? In these circumstances can the ordination of women ever be discussed at all in the future in an ecumenical context? Whereas official Roman Catholic voices regularly state that the ordination of women is an obstacle to ecumenical dialogue, many Roman Catholic laity and theologians welcome the introduction of the ordination of women by other Christian churches. This is clear from the reaction to the priestly ordination of women in the Anglican and Old Catholic churches in recent years. The readiness to accept women into the ministry has settled in the hearts and minds of many Christians in recent decades.

Is the ordination of women a sign of the time? For Giuseppe Ruggieri, signs of the time are processes which enter the general consciousness and lead to a shift of human relations in a messianic direction in a particular era.[1] Signs of the time are infectious and in a particular era take on collective significance. They put continuity in question, mark turning points in history and allow unexpected things to happen. In signs of the time, God's kingdom becomes present among men and women; they contribute towards the humanization of men and women in the light of the gospel. The church has the task of recognizing the signs of the time at the right moment, interpreting them and discovering in them the message of the gospel for today.

May the question of the ordination of women be connected with signs of our time, in this case specifically with the modern movement for the emancipation of women? Anyone who immediately conjures up the caricature that feminists are now finally storming the last male bastion falls short of the mark. From such a perspective emancipation is too quickly dismissed as a secular movement which is incompatible with a sacramental order. The rediscovery of the biblical category of 'signs of the time' as a principle for the theological interpretation of reality is one of the most important results of John XXIII's reform programme: after Vatican II the words 'secular' and 'worldly' can no longer be used in their old meanings.[2]

The spirit of Vatican II and the new departure for women

During his time in office Pope John XXIII showed great openness to modern developments in society. The assessment of the movement of the emancipation for women as a 'sign of the time' in the encyclical *Pacem in Terris* (1963) was a hopeful beginning in integrating the question of women as a question for the church. The Pastoral Constitution *Gaudium et Spes* condemned any form of discrimination on the basis of sex, race, colour of skin, class, language or religion (no. 29). The Council did not accept the demand for equal rights for women in the church and their admission to all offices, which was made in various petitions to it; however, various conciliar declarations proved stimuli to a reform of the position of women in the church.[3] The Council opened doors which were partly closed again under the successors to John XXIII; the conflict was already apparent then in some compromise formulae of the Council. However, the spirit of openness and a new departure for women was unstoppable: the Council 'spoke with a new voice and with new enthusiasm about discerning the signs of the times'.[4] It is this spirit which in the eyes of other churches really makes Vatican II, which was a Roman Catholic 'general synod of the bishops and their dioceses allied with the pope',[5] a *kairos* in twentieth-century church history.

Since then much has happened within the churches, theology and among women themselves to keep the question of women alive in the church's consciousness and to contribute towards awareness of it. In the course of this growing awareness the demand for the ordination of women has made itself heard increasingly persistently and loudly in various churches. Far-reaching social changes in the course of this century have contributed to the change in perceived values and careers for women and have resulted in possibilities of real participation by women beyond the 'classic' roles assigned to them. The present-day discussion about the ordination of women is to be located in this modern landscape in church and society. The issue is to incorporate and make fruitful the competences and charisms of women by incorporating them into the church's ordained ministry. The experiences of women are visibly and audibly to enter the ministry of the proclamation of the good news of Christ. Women in the ordained ministry symbolize the change from the woman as an object of preaching to its subject. So it is no coincidence that the present-day debate on the ordination of women often concentrates on the '*repraesentatio Christi*'. It is an important insight, grounded in soteriology, that women can be icons of the Incarnate, since they are redeemed as women. The issue here is the authoritative representation of Christ by women. The discussion in the early church and the Middle Ages about whether women can possess and exercise spiritual authority, which at that time was answered in the negative for the female sex as a whole, is being continued under the conditions of modern society. So the ordination of women has, not least, become the symbol of the question of women in the church generally, because in the meantime the capacity of women to exercise authority is unquestionable in the present-day cultural environment and on the basis of more recent insights of biblical theology.[6] That removes the main traditional argument against the ordination of women. It must rightly be asked on what grounds the conclusions which have been drawn from this argument for centuries continue to be maintained.

For any church which has gone through the discussion over the ordination of women, it has been exhausting and revealing. Statements which are apparently friendly towards women are unmasked as a subtle continuation of subordinationist thinking, which one had believed already to have been superseded; traditional models of perception collided with models for describing the relationship between the sexes which were based more on partnership. More than other topics, the discussion of the ordination of women has taken the churches to the abysses of their own more or less hidden ecclesiastical misogyny and disclosed everyday sexism. At the same time unexpected and untrodden paths which are also offered by the Christian tradition, or paths which had been grown over, have been taken or opened up again. In this way the rediscovery of the Christian tradition of women supplements and corrects one-sidedly androcentric strands of tradition.[7]

The ordination of women as an ecumenical task

It is often said that the ordination of women is a challenge. This word is popular usage in diplomatic ecumenical language. It can serve to disguise the intentions of the speaker, for what represents a 'provocation' to some is a problem for others and a task for yet others. A further difficulty is that in practice the meanings exclude one another: anyone who perceives the ordination of women from the aspect of provocation is usually not inclined to undertake the ordination of women as a task. But that is precisely what is necessary today. No church will be able to evade this task in the long run, since in contemporary discussion it is very closely interwoven with the question of women generally.

The ordination of women as a task is generally regarded as a question which can only finally be resolved in the future, and then by an ecumenical council. This argument can be misused to postpone an answer to the question for ever. However, its urgency and relevance already requires it to be discussed today in a way which does justice to our state of theological knowledge and the life of the church in the local communities. A categorical 'no' or a ban on discussion will hardly be able to stop the discussion; it merely complicates the situation, since within Roman Catholicism obedience to the magisterium is now also brought into play.[8]

It is probably no coincidence that it is mainly women who put the ordination of women in the sphere of ecumenical tasks which need to be tackled today.[9] For many of them, the ordination of women has become the touchstone for the way in which churches deal with the question of women in the church and the participation and shared responsibility of church members.

Whereas thirty years ago it was still the spokespersons of women's ordination who had to support their position with arguments, now the burden of proof is with their opponents.[10] For a long time the discussion over the ordination of women has ceased to be a discussion in an academic ivory tower; women's ordination has become conceivable for many people living today. 'Become conceivable': these two words indicate what an enormous change in consciousness has taken place over the capacity of women to hold office in the church. And why should not the ordination of women be capable of integration into any church tradition and essence? In the sphere of practical coexistence and at the level of theological discussion, ecumenical openness during this century has brought the churches closer in a way which is proving fruitful particularly in the question of the ordination of women. As by coming to know one another in ecumenical collaboration men, and to an even greater degree women, share comparable experiences, 'constellations of solidarity' have come into being which transcend confessions.[11] They are not to be underestimated. This is becoming clear for example in the ready acceptance of Anglican and Old Catholic women priests as representatives of a *Catholic* ordained ministry among Roman Catholic men and women. The churches have also borrowed from each other in theological discussions for or against the ordination of women to support their own particular arguments. This happens, for example, in the case of the argument over the *repraesentatio Christi* in the discussion in Western Catholic churches and the character of the priest as an icon on the Orthodox side, of which there is no evidence as an argument in the discussion in the early church. The same goes for the biblical argument for and against, which was first worked out by the Protestant churches and then taken up and reflected upon again by other churches in which the discussion began at a later stage in time.

Theological reflection on the ordination of women and its subsequent introduction has been fruitful in many respects. That is shown, for example, by the appeal to scripture and tradition in connection with the question whether their testimony is used openly to ward off the question, or tradition is regarded as a 'river of life':[12] a process of creative, living translation from which new answers can be given to today's questions. That the appeal to the Bible alone is not sufficient argument against the ordination of women is evident from the opening up of the ordained ministry to women in the Protestant churches. In 1976 the Papal Biblical Commission also came to the conclusion that biblical grounds alone were insufficient for excluding the ordination of women.[13] Tradition cannot be a closed treasure chest; it is a dowry which only brings riches when it is handed on. A further yield of the discussion over the ordination of women is that it has led to deepened reflection on the significance and exercise of the church's ministries within the communities.[14] The pneumatological aspect has also gained ground as a supplement to the christocentric basis in the theology of the ministry.

Where some fear that the ordained ministry is losing part of its mystical character as the priestly office, others experience the incorporation of women as an enrichment of the priestly office and a spiritual deepening with which the saving mission of Christ is also expressed in the structure of the ministries. The experience of those churches which see themselves as Catholic and have called women to the ordained ministry is that their Catholicity has been deepened in a special way through the incorporation of ordained women ministers: being Catholic also means being related to *all* men and women.[15]

To sum up: it can be said that churches which have grappled with the ordination of women have been stimulated to examine critically their theological understanding of themselves as churches.

The ordination of women: a test case for conciliarity

Given such a gain as a consequence of grappling with the ordination of women, the charge that ecumenism will be burdened or hampered by the introduction of the ordination of women is all the more serious. By it women are implicitly being made the scapegoats for a problem which really concerns the churches themselves. Moreover this view takes in only one part of the present-day ecumenical landscape. For in ecumenism as practised in the local churches and in women's ecumenism, women in the ordained ministry are not seen as an obstacle but more as companions and mediators of a more human church, a church which takes form in a true community of women and men.

In the discussion over the ordination of women in the Old Catholic Churches of the Utrecht Union which has been taking place over the last twenty-five years, the question of decision-making kept arising. Is it possible to introduce the priestly ordination of women despite a contrary practice over nineteen centuries? People were clear that the ordination of women was really a task to be resolved by a truly ecumenical council. However, at present the expectation of such a council is unrealistic. But that does not mean that it is impossible already to practise conciliarity now. There should be ecumenical consultations over questions which are controversial today, consultations which reflect on their sources and the common origin of the churches. The aim of the quest for the common faith which exists beyond the historic frontiers of churches and confessions is to discuss together 'how the traditions can be developed without losing the common tradition'.[16] This process of conciliar discovery should be understood as an open quest which does not know the answers in advance or fix labels on others like 'Protestantizing' or 'liberalizing'. Thus conciliarity is to be understood as the readiness to join in a shared process of learning, to engage in a search for what binds the churches together in the light of their common origin and for how tradition is realized in the light of present circumstances and demands. It means discussing with one another and sharing insights, anxieties and experiences with one another. Conciliarity means that voices from all the church people are heard, that the silent testimony of theologians condemned to dumbness also finds a hearing. Granted, a conciliarity of this kind would not have any legally binding authority. But does not the discussion over the ordination of women in particular show more than any other the failure of authoritatively prescribed solutions? Unless preceded by a 'conciliar process', no authoritative decision on this question is credible, whereas the church authorities gain high moral authority from a conciliar consultation. It is here above all that I see the decisive unanswered question which stood at the head of this article. The way in which the tension between conciliarity and authoritative decision is resolved is decisive both for the further discussion of the question of women within each church and for ecumenical relations between the churches.

Translated by John Bowden

Notes

1. See his contribution in this issue.
2. Lavinia Byrne, *Women at the Altar. The Ordination of Women in the Roman Catholic Church*, London 1994, 17: 'Suddenly the words secular and worldly cannot be used with their old meanings.'
3. Ida Raming, *Frauenbewegung und Kirche. Bilanz eines 25jährigen Kampfes für Gleichberechtigung und Befreiung der Frau seit dem 2. Vatikanischen Konzil,* Weinheim 1989, 26–41.
4. Bryne, *Woman at the Altar* (n.1), 15.
5. *Internationale Kirchliche Zeitschrift* 60, 1970, 161.
6. Here in particular the affirmation that women are completely in the image of God plays an important role. See Kari Elisabeth Børreson, 'The Ordination of Women: To Nurture Tradition by Continuing Inculturation', *Studia Theologica* 46, 1992, 3–13.
7. Cf. Elisabeth Gössmann, 'Frauentraditionen im Christentum in ihrer Relevanz für heutige Feministische Theologie und in ihrer kirchlichen Einschätzung', in E. Hartlieb and C. Methuen (eds), *Sources and Resources of Feminist Theologies*, ESWTR Yearbook 5, Kampen and Mainz 1997, 72–95.
8. Hedwig Meyer-Wilmes, 'Zum Dienst ermächtigt. Amtsformen zwischen Tradition und Moderne', in Marianne Bühle, Brigitte Enzner-Probst, Hedwig Meyer-Wilmes and Hanneliese Steichele, *Frauen zwischen Dienst und Arnt. Frauenmacht und -ohnmacht in der Kirche,* Düsseldorf 1998, 85–114: 88.
9. Anne Jensen, 'Ist Frauenordination ein ökumenisches Problem? Zu den jüngsten Entwicklungen in den anglikanischen, altkatholischen und Orthodoxen Kirchen', *Internationale Kirchliche Zeitschrift* 84, 1994, 210–28; a shorter revised version appeared in *Theologische Quartalschrift* 173, 1993, 236–41.
10. Ibid., 241.
11. Marianne Heimbach-Steins, 'Frauenbild und Frauenrolle. Gesellschaftliche und kirchliche Leitideen im Hintergrund der Diskussion um den Diakonat der

Frau', in Peter Hünermann et al. (eds), *Diakonat. Ein Amt für Frauen in der Kirche – ein frauengerechtes Amt?*, Ostfildern 1997, 14–32: 21.

12. Elisabeth Behr-Sigel, *The Ministry of Women in the Church*, Redondo Beach 1987, 94.

13. Raming, *Frauenbewegung* (n.2), 45.

14. Jensen, 'Frauenordination' (n.9)., 222.

15. Joachim Vobbe, *Geh zu meinen Brudern. Vom priesterlichen Auftrag der Frauen in der Kirche. Brief des Bischofs an die Gemeinden des Katholischen Bistums der Alt-Katholiken*, Bonn 1996, 28.

16. Jan Visser, 'Die Frage der Frauenordination und die Gemeinschaft der Kirchen', *Internationale Kirchliche Zeitschrift* 88, 1998, 329–44: 341. The paper was given in 1996 at the 'Orthodox – Old Catholic Consultation on the Status of Women in the Church and the Ordination of Women as an Ecumenical Problem'. The papers were edited by Urs von Arx and Anastasios Kallis under the title *Bild Christi und Geschlecht* (ibid., 67–348). The participants in the consultation arrived at the common conviction 'that there are no compelling dogmatic and theological reasons why women should not be ordained to the priestly ministry' (ibid., 82).

Theology of Mission or of Missions? The Treatment of a Controversial Term

Giancarlo Collet

The Second Vatican Council showed a resolutely missionary attitude by asking about the self-understanding of the church and its task in the light of the present world situation. Even if at that time the world situation was still predominantly perceived from a European perspective and the documents which were approved are stamped with European theology, this does not alter the fact that this Council, as Karl Rahner put it, 'is the beginning of a tentative approach by the church to the discovery and official realization of itself as *world-church*'.[1] After a very brief period of Jewish Christianity characterized by the proclamation of the gospel 'within its own historical situation (not in any other situation) following the decision in Jerusalem, there was a transition from a Jewish Christianity to a Christianity of the Gentiles as such. This second period, which lasted for centuries, was characterized 'by a particular cultural group, that of Hellenism and European culture and civilization'. For the third period, beginning with Vatican II, 'the church's living space is from the very outset the whole world'.[2]

Vatican II also represents an important milestone in the development of the theology of mission, in that here a beginning was made on a theology of mission which all over the world reminded each local church that it was the subject of evangelization, as distinct from a theology which still saw missionary activity exclusively as the work of European churches in distant lands under the supervision of Rome. This was connected on the one hand with the changed situation of the world church and on the other with the newly-gained self-understanding of the church. In the meantime, independent local churches had developed from the so-called mission churches, and these claimed the right to their own expression of faith. They saw themselves challenged – not least in the course of the general process of emancipation from Western rule – to redefine their place within their particular societies and to set their own tasks.

The missionary activity of the Christian faith-communities had always been carried on in the light of a particular understanding of themselves and of the world and the people to whom the gospel was to be preached. However, not only the churches' understanding of themselves but also the understanding of the world and the relationship between the two have changed in the course of history.[3] One need only refer to the study *The Church for Others*, a report by the World Council of Churches on proclaiming the gospel, which rethought the relationship between the church and the world and produced the formula 'The world sets the agenda' to indicate the historical change in the definition of the relationship between the church and the world.[4] The rise of numerous contextual theologies in Third World countries which began from analyses of particular situations in order to be able to present the gospel appropriately to the people living there as the 'word of life' is also an expression of a new definition of the relationship between church and world; of course this also sparked off theological discussions and led to tensions between the churches.

The following remarks attempt to show briefly how in the development of the magisterium since the passing of the Decree on Mission at the Council there is an increasing 'openness' in the definition of the concept of mission which on the one hand helps towards a comprehensive, holistic understanding of the task of the church, but which on the other can also still be used for a geographically restricted view of mission. So at present there are also two contrary tendencies in the theology of mission. Whereas one is strongly bound up with Western traditions and their 'conceptual theology', the other, starting from a variety of experiences in different cultural and religious situations, is trying to work out a theology of mission which can be described as contextual.

I. Mission or missions of the church?

As is well known, the Decree on the Missionary Activity of the Church had an eventful prehistory.[5] Different versions were rejected by relevant commissions because they treated the theme one-sidedly from disciplinary, pastoral and canonistic perspectives. Proposals for reform contained in the drafts also came up against opposition. A more decidedly theological treatment of the problem was called for by the Council fathers. Moreover what the Council finally approved was a 'compromise paper', which became a correction, but not a 'Magna Carta', of mission.[6]

Whereas the original document still spoke of the one mission, at the last minute the term 'missions' (in the plural) was reintroduced, so that the theological result achieved, which spoke of the one mission of Christ and his church in terms of a universal and global understanding of mission, was at least indirectly put in question, if not withdrawn again. The statement that the whole church is missionary, and that mission therefore belongs to the essence of the church, is fundamental to the understanding of the Decree on Mission *Ad Gentes* (cf. AG 2), which has to be seen and understood in connection with the Constitution on the Church, *Lumen Gentium;* the Pastoral Constitution, *Gaudium et Spes;* and the Declaration on the Non-Christian Religions, *Nostra Aetate.* As the church sent into the world, the church has to bear witness to the salvation established by Christ; it is the 'comprehensive sacrament of salvation' (LG 48, AF 1).

However, the very first chapter, which is concerned with the theological foundation of mission, makes the conceptual division indicated above quite clear. Whereas to begin with mission meant the one mission of the church in its various functions, AG 6 immediately speaks of missions as 'special undertakings in which preachers of the Gospel, sent by the Church, and going into the whole world, carry out the work of preaching the Gospel and implanting the Church among people who do not yet believe in Christ'. No theological reason is recognizable here for clarifying the unity of the mission of the church and the missions and the differences between them. Rather, on the basis of external conditions and those to whom it is addressed, the one mission of the church comes to be differentiated in a way which geographical, chronological and socio-cultural perspectives are introduced to explain. So two different ways of speaking of mission are clear in the Decree on Mission: on the one hand the Council presents an understanding of the church which defines mission as a *function of the essence* of the church and as a task shared by the whole church. But on the other, a view can be recognized according to which mission represents a *special activity* of the church. This 'ambiguity' in the term mission also subsequently allowed different interpretations.

II. Evangelization – a new key concept

The Apostolic Exhortation of Paul VI, *Evangelii Nuntiandi*, which appeared ten years after the end of the Council, formed an important milestone in the development of the theology of mission. This took up the Synod of Bishops held the previous year. 'Unlike the Second Vatican Council, and more markedly than the previous Synods of Bishops, the

Synod of 1974 was an event at which the young churches of Africa, Asia and Latin America had a voice. They governed ways of thinking, language and themes as never before. In fact here for the first time the end of the Eurocentric epoch of church history became evident and at the same time the end of the history of theology orientated on the classics.'[7] The Exhortation stated that: 'Evangelizing is in fact the grace and vocation proper to the church, her deepest identity' (EN 14). The very choice of terminology and the theological approach are remarkable. Whereas the Council had already spoken of evangelization – the word occurs thirty-one times in all in the documents – at that time it was not yet able to establish the term. Things are different in *Evangelii Nuntiandi*, which uses the term mission very sparsely[8] and makes evangelization a key term. Even the concept of mission used in *Ad Gentes* is superseded when in EN 17 it is stated: 'Any partial and fragmentary definition which attempts to render the reality of evangelization in all its richness, complexity and dynamism does so only at the risk of impoverishing it and even of distorting it. It is impossible to grasp the concept of evangelization unless one tries to keep in view all its essential elements.'

With evangelization, not only was a new concept of the theology of mission introduced into the vocabulary of the magisterium, but an attempt was also made to systematize linguistically the various activities of the mission of the church. Here the term is to be understood comprehensively. The sense in which this is intended becomes clear from EN 19 when it is said: 'For the Church it is a question not only of preaching the Gospel in ever wider geographic areas or to ever greater numbers of people, but also of affecting and as it were upsetting, through the power of the Gospel, mankind's criteria of judgment, determining values, points of interest, lines of thought, sources of inspiration and models of life, which are in contrast with the word of God and the plan of salvation.'

If the Decree on Mission still determined missionary action as a 'purely religious, supernatural activity', a clear change becomes evident in this document, in that it undertakes a comprehensive description of the mission of the church, a constitutive element in which is dedication to the liberation of men and women (EN 30). It is important to fight against injustice and to restore justice (EN 31). 'For the church, evangelizing (accordingly) means bringing the Good News into all the strata of humanity, and through its influence transforming humanity from within and making it new' (EN 18).

III. Mission *ad gentes* – a return to the missions?

John Paul's 1990 encyclical on mission, *Redemptoris Missio*, refers back to the Missionary Decree *Ad Gentes* and to the Apostolic Exhortation *Evangelii Nuntiandi*, and presents a clearly defined concept of mission.[9] The document emphasizes 'that the whole church is a missionary church' (RM 31), 'missionary by nature' (RM 62). At the same time, however, the encyclical indicates that this statement does not preclude 'the existence of a specific mission *ad gentes*' (RM 32), which is 'one of the Church's fundamental activities' that 'is essential and never-ending' (RM 31). Thus John Paul II maintains the one mission of the church – 'Mission is a single but complex reality' (RM 41) – but at the same time emphasizes the differences in the activity which arise 'from the variety of circumstances in which that mission is carried on' (RM 33).

Redemptoris Missio lists three different spheres for the mission *ad gentes*. First, mention is made of territorial limits or a geographical criterion: 'The growth in the number of new Churches in recent times should not deceive us. Within the territories entrusted to these Churches – particularly in Asia, but also in Africa, Latin America and Oceania – there remain vast regions still to be evangelized' (RM 37a). Secondly, mention is made of new worlds and new social phenomena: 'Today the image of mission *ad gentes* is perhaps changing: efforts should be concentrated on the big cities, where new customs and styles of living arise together with new forms of culture and communication, which then influence the wider population' (RM 37b). Finally the document speaks of cultural sectors, the modern equivalents of the Areopagus; the world of communications, scholarly research and international relations (RM 37c).

Within the framework of the one mission of the church the document finally describes three situations which govern different activities: 1. The mission *ad gentes* proper; 2. pastoral activity; and 3. new evangelization. Although the pope declares that 'the boundaries between pastoral care of the faithful, new evangelization and specific missionary activity cannot clearly be defined' (RM 34), and accordingly that the terms cannot simply be assigned to more geographical spheres, this in fact happens in the further description of these situations. In the encyclical the term mission is in fact used in both a strictly theological and also again in a geographical sense.[10]

IV. Towards an integral understanding of mission

If we compare the more recent documents on the theology of mission from world Christianity with those sketched out here, another, more sober, picture emerges, because these documents always begin from real situations in which the churches find themselves, and derive a concept of mission from them.[11] In the vast majority of cases the starting point is the visible, empirical form of the church, and the world is similarly perceived from a concrete standpoint. The concern is with existing social conditions, cultural and religious traditions which can be made the point of reference for theological reflection on the mission of the church. In this way such documents make it clear that missionary activity never takes place in an abstract 'world' but in a multiplicity of different contexts, and accordingly also shows a broad spectrum of forms of missionary expression. Therefore mission is no longer limited to the proclamation of the gospel, church implanting, the extension of the church, conversion, etc., but embraces a shaping of the 'world' which is expressed with terms like 'total liberation' or 'comprehensiveness'.

Such an integral understanding of mission overcomes the polarizations which keep emerging in the debate on mission, for example in questions of the status of preaching and social action. According to an integral understanding of mission which is formulated on the basis of the answer to be given to the 'signs of the time', there can be no prior hierarchy, but it is possible to start from a mutual combination of items of equal importance. Over and above this, such an understanding overcomes the separation of 'inner mission', or evangelizing or re-evangelizing among the baptized, and 'outside mission' among those who have not been baptized; finally, it makes a one-sidedly geographical fixation on 'the trans-cultural mission of the West overseas' obsolete.[12] Certainly the missionary task sets any church against a universal horizon, but that church is first of all sent to the people in its own context. The local churches bear a special responsibility for this mission.

In the methodological approach in which a theology of mission is being worked out today, first of all a notable difference from the documents of the magisterium is developing. Not only is the variety of contextually conditioned experiences being made the starting point for reflection on Christian faith instead of theological documents which are handed down or fixed concepts; in addition there is an emphasis on a plurality in the theological mission which is dictated by the situation. The 'missionary consciousness' of the churches of the South since the beginning of the 1970s is striking when compared with the churches of the North, and a centuries-old monopoly of interpretation of the Christian message by the West European churches is being rejected. And the more strongly the churches of the South take the missionary task into their own hands, the more the churches of the North will be subjected to critical questioning. Here one notes with surprise: 'The more critical the questions asked about the classic understanding of mission are . . . the greater has mutual fruitfulness become in thought about the theology of mission. The general "crisis in mission" is matched by a hitherto unknown openness and acceptance of reflection on the theology of mission in other confessional families."[13]

One of the open questions not only of a theology of mission but also of theology generally is what an intercultural hermeneutic would look like which took seriously the appropriation and developed interpretation of the gospel in a particular context, and at the same time held fast to the universality of the one truth of faith and the one church.[14] The more the church really becomes the world church, the more varied Christianity will also become, and the more urgent the answer to this question will be.

Translated by John Bowden

Notes

1. K. Rahner, 'Basic Theological Interpretation of the Second Vatican Council', in *Theological Investigations* 10, London 1981, 77–89: 78; cf. id., 'The Abiding Significance of the Second Vatican Council', in ibid., 90–102: 91. Cf. O. H. Pesch, *Das Zweite Vatikanische Konzil. Vorgeschichte – Verlauf – Ergebnisse – Nachgeschichte*, Würzburg 1994, 359ff.

2. Rahner, 'Basic Theological Interpretation' (n.1), 83.

3. S. Dianich, *Chiesa in missione. Per una ecclesiologia dinamica*, Milan 1987, 40–79; id., *Chiesa estroversa. Una ricerca sulla svolta dell' ecclesiologia contemporanea*, Milan 1987: D. J. Bosch, *Transforming Mission. Paradigm Shifts in Theology of Mission*, Maryknoll 1991, esp. 181ff., with the corresponding Reader, *Classic Texts in Mission and World Christianity*, ed. N. E. Thomas. Maryknoll 1995, esp. Part I.

4. *The Church for Others and the Church for the World. Final Report of the Western European and North American Working Parties on the Report for Questions of Proclamation*, Geneva 1967, esp. 19ff.; cf. W. Simpfendörfer, *Kirchenreform 1, Die Gemeinde vor der Tagesordnung der Welt. Dokumente und Entwürfe*, Stuttgart 1968; id., *Offene Kirche – kritische Kirche. Kirchenreform am Scheidewege*, Stuttgart and Berlin 1969, esp. 9ff.

5. Vgl. J. Glazik, 'Vor 25 Jahren Missionsdekret "Ad Gentes". Erinnerungen eines Augenzeugen des Konzils', in *Zeitschrift für Missionswissenschaft und Religionswissenschaft* 74, 1990, 257–74.

6. J. Glazil, 'Eine Korrektur. Keine Magna Charta', in *Die Autorität der Freiheit. Gegenwart des Konzils und Zukunft der Kirche im ökumenischen Disput*, ed. J. C. Hampe, Vol. 3, Munich 1967, 543–53.

7. H. J. Pottmeyer, 'Kontextualität und Pluralität. Die Bischofssynode von 1974', *Theologie und Glaube* 86, 1996, 167–80: 167.

8. Cf. F. Kollbrunner, 'Missionstheoretische Überlegungen zu *Evangelii Nuntiandi*', *Neue Zeitschrift für Missionswissenschaft* 32, 1976, 242–54: 243.

9. Cf. J. Neuner, 'Mission in *Ad Gentes* and in *Redemptoris Missio*', *Vidyajyoti. Journal of Theological Reflection* 56, 1992, 228–41: P. Tihon, 'Retour aux missions?

Une lecture de l' encyclique "Redemptoris Missio"', *Nouvelle Revue Théologique* 114, 1992, 69–86; W. Hering, 'Schon wieder ein neuer Missionsbegriff?', *Lebendiges Zeugnis* 47, 1992, 117–24; H. Rzepkowski, 'Neue Perspektiven und Probleme des Missionsbegriffes. Zur Missionsenzyklika "Redemptoris Missio"', *Forum katholische Theologie* 9, 1993, 194–213.

10. Cf. E. Nunnenmacher, '"Le Missioni" – un concetto vacillante riabilitato? Riflessioni sulla dimensione geografica di un termine classico', *Euntes docete* 44, 1991, 241–64.

11. Cf. M. R. Spindler, 'Mission Reaffirmed: Recent Authoritative Statements of Churches Around the World (1982–1991)', *Exchange* 20, 1991, 161–258; J. A. Scherer and S. B. Bevans, *New Directions in Mission and Evangelization I: Basic Statements 1974–1991*, Maryknoll 1992; id., *Theological Foundations*, Maryknoll 1994; J. Wietzke (ed), *Mission erklärt. Ökumenische Dokumente von 1972 bis 1992*, Leipzig 1993.

12. Cf. H. W. Gensichen, 'Akzente und Problemstellungen in der gegenwärtigen evangelischen Missionstheologie', *Zeitschrift für Missionswissenschaft und Religionswissenschaft* 75, 1986, 112–27: 122.

13. J. Wietzke, 'Auswertender Rückblick', in *Mission erklärt* (n. 22), 426.

14. Cf. D. Mieth, E. Schillebeeckx and H. Snijdewind (eds), *Cammino e visione. Universalità e gerinalità della teologia nel XX secolo. Scritti in onore di Rosino Gibbelini*, Brescia 1996; M. Bongard, 'Glaubenseinheit statt Einheitsglaube. Zu Anliegen und Problematik kontextueller Theologien', in K. Müller (ed.), *Fundamentaltheologie – Fluchtlinien und gegenwärtige Herausforderungen*, Regensburg 1998, 243–60.

Church, Modernity and Postmodernity

Maureen Junker-Kenny

The title of many of the short articles in this issue, taking stock of the century of the Second Vatican Council, may sound comprehensive, and the selection made must necessarily be limited; however, the brief from the editors indicates both an approach and a hope for coherence: 'How does the article fit into an overall scheme of theology? In what way is it representative? What alternatives does it present?' Since on postmodern premises the first question of an 'overall scheme' may already be regarded as the symptom of a unifying thought which needs to be overcome, it can only be discussed in second place, in the context of the investigation of the alleged opposition between modernity and postmodernity and its consequences for theology. The second question, namely in what way the article is representative, rather than being random, arbitrary or marginal, offers the way in. It is representative in making the disputed signature of the time itself the topic, just as Christian Duquoc's article 'Faith in a Time of Cultural Amnesia', Karl-Josef Kuschel's article 'Aesthetic Culture as a Secular Religion?', and Felix Wilfred's article 'A New Way of Being Christians' describe contemporary conditions for faith. The third question, about alternatives, first emerges in Part II, to the extent that this investigates the alternatives of modernity and postmodernity, and then above all in Part III, 'Questions to the churches', which is principally orientated on praxis.

I. The difficulty of diagnosing the time

Ulrich Barth indicates the difficulties of making diagnoses of the time. Unlike medical diagnoses, these cannot base their findings on any assured knowledge of the normal and the healthy.

Those who make a diagnosis of the time must rather identify given situations without having available to them a physiology or pathology of social developments. They are therefore forced to combine with the analysis of particular phenomena the discovery of overarching tendencies against the background of which these phenomena can first be described. Here the specification of individual details coincides with the reconstruction of a general picture. In other words, the identification made by the subsuming power of judgment and the contribution of the reflective power of judgment to a definition are mutually dependent on each other . . . Precisely for that reason any attempt to diagnose the time has more or less the character of divination.[1]

Schleiermacher used this concept in his hermeneutics to emphasize that any attempt at mutual understanding had the character of a provisional scheme which is then examined by the comparative method. The particular problem of a diagnosis of the present, that it has to define the general at the same time as the particular, forms a precise parallel to Schleiermacher's remarks about the way in which children learn language: they have to discover the contextual significance of a meaning and the general scheme at the same time. It is this capacity for an original production of meaning which first creates the possibility of comparison.[2]

Applied to the demarcation between modernity and postmodernity, a recognition of the divinatory element in a diagnosis of the time means that the individual observation has to be referred back to the overall scheme, and the descriptive analysis to the programme. Thus already within the theories of modernization it is striking how in European analyses all the attention is directed towards the reasons for individualization, the way in which it appears and its consequences, and the remaining collective references like the 'communities of origin' from which language and forms of cultural behaviour, social standards and binding myths stem, which are important for North American investigations, fade into the background. Whether the diagnosis of the present as 'postmodern' is presented as a programme or descriptively, with attention to subtle differences and shifts of accent, the result is that the relationship between modernity and postmodernity appears either as a break or, in continuity, as an ongoing development with radicalized determinations. Both stop at the negative self-determination 'post-' and fail to give a positive description of the content of the new era; however, the substance of this latter is close to the theoreticians of 'late modernity' or 'modernity which has come to reflect on itself'. The real point of dispute in this intellectual, political and theological self-location lies in the question of the normative content of modernity, which is either to be destroyed or to be continued critically in the face of new challenges.

II. Modernity – postmodernity: the content of the opposition and its consequences for theology

How one relates to modernity, whether and how one postulates post-modernity at the same time, has both consequences for and foundations in the overall scheme of theology. Whether there are alternatives is decided by what has to be overcome: 1. The great narratives; 2. Logo-centrism and the notion of presence; 3. Unitary thinking; 4. The concept of the subject and the idea of freedom.

1. Presumably no theological approach can adopt the programme of what Lyotard has called 'the end of the great narratives', even if theological reasons could be adduced for now playing down the concept of 'salvation history' which since Irenaeus has become central, in view of the experience of the Holocaust and given the existence of peoples who have only been embraced by Christianity in modern times.[3] Belief in creation and redemption and the hope for final meaning are so essential to the Christian understanding of God that, quite apart from the question of their anthropological relevance, if Christianity put an end to this narrative, it would give itself up.

2. In a more recent attempt at theological mediation, on the one hand the motifs of Jacques Derrida's criticism of logocentrism and the notion of presence have been developed and applied to traditions in Christianity like negative theology, though on the other hand they have identified the point of conflict. Derrida's concept of scripture is explained against the background of the rabbinic interpretation of the Torah: 'The open pluralism of the most different kinds of reading not only keeps alive the awareness of the ineffability of the NAME but at the same time is an exercise in the perception of the other (here the interpreter).'[4] At the same time Valentine also makes theological use of an argument produced by philosophers: 'Theological discourse could be . . . particularly affected by an unrestrained "critique of totality", since as far as it is concerned a metaphysical remnant continues to be indispensable – because of the unconditional claim which it sets out to present, e.g. an underived concept of identity.'[5] The Tübingen philosopher Hans Krämer gives the following analysis in his critique of 'radical hermeneu-tic' positions, i.e. those 'which increasingly eliminate the substratum of interpretation and tend towards a self-accomplishment of the event of interpretation: . . . Even the radical hermeneutic of Derrida and de Man,

which holds that it is impossible to decide between infinite possibilities of interpretation even in the individual case, concedes a minimal identity between the presence of the world and the self. Otherwise, his kind of hermeneutic generalizes a particular type of a failure to understand and misunderstanding, and thus establishes a counter-metaphysic to the traditional metaphysic of unity and identity, which is just as selective and stylizes just as dogmatically as that does.'[6] From a philosophical and theological perspective, the postmodern abandonment of the concept of identity is problematical.

3. Jürgen Habermas, himself a critic of the metaphysic of identity, takes up the postmodern criticism of the notion of unity with an insight into the relationship between opposite poles, which is explained as partly dialectical and partly transcendental:

> The horrified rejection of the one and the praise of difference and of the other obscure the dialectical connection between the two. For the transitory unity which is produced in the porous and broken intersubjectivity of a linguistically communicated consensus not only guarantees the pluralization of forms of life and the individualization of life-style but furthers and accelerates. The more discussion, the more contradiction and difference. The more abstract the agreement, the more manifold the dissents with which we can live in a non-violent way. Yet in public awareness the consequence of a compulsive integration of the many is associated with the idea of unity. Moral universalism is still regarded as an enemy of individualism, not as something that makes it possible. The attribution of identical meanings is still regarded as a violation of metaphorical ambiguity, not as its condition. The unity of reason is still regarded as repression, not as the source of the multiplicity of its voices. The false suggestions of a unitary thought said good-bye to one hundred and fifty years ago still form the background – as if today, like the first generation of pupils of Hegel, we still had to defend ourselves against the superior power of the great metaphysical masters.[7]

In this way Habermas uses basic concepts of modernity (unity, agreement, universalism, reason) as a condition for the possibility of the postulated postmodern content (difference and others, dissent and plurality).

Since the controversies over Pelagius, Erasmus and Luther, and Modernism, the theological critics of modern freedom of thought can rely on an orthodox tail wind which goes beyond the confessions. For them, farewells to the subject and reason are no great loss, and the task and categories of mediation with philosophical thought of no interest. By contrast, with the departure from modernity, theological projects aware of their obligations to the anthropological shift to subjectivity have lost the decisive category for expounding the self-revelation of God in the person of Jesus: unconditional mutual recognition as a free event. Whether this normative core of the project of modernity is abandoned, or retained and made concrete, will decide the humane and Christian acceptability of postmodernity.[8] In an interview, J.-F. Lyotard makes clear his support for this ethical orientation. He condemns:

> acting in accordance with a principle which consists in not accepting the other as a partner in the conversation. 'I'm not talking to you!' The equivalent happens in every school playground: 'I'm not playing with you!' The contempt, the ostracism, is a crime against humanity. One is denying someone the right to speak the moment when he has the capacity to speak. My view on this is . . . not far removed from that which Habermas or Rorty may have for quite different motives and which they arrive at for quite different reasons.

Unlike Levinas or even Habermas, Lyotard emphasizes the ambivalence of the encounter with the other, which first makes his demand for the recognition of the right of the stranger significant:

> The relationship to the stranger is necessarily ambivalent, since on the one hand as a human being he can talk and discuss, is capable of being an 'interlocutor' in the broadest sense of the word; and his right to this must be recognized. However, on the other hand he speaks his own language . . . Someone is a stranger to the degree that I find no access to the logic of his language and it seems to me . . . as if he has another heritage, as if on his lips even my own language is saying something different, as if here there was an occasion for mistrust. At a descriptive level, the idea that one receives a stranger with open arms is a somewhat strange notion. However, in concepts of justice it is not only desirable but in fact requisite. By contrast, at a descriptive level it is simply not true that this is the case. Rather, there is something here which in Freudian terms one would call a destructive drive . . . in relation to what disrupts my environment, damages its stability, to what threatens me . . . The real question is how that can be overcome. The definition of alterity lies in the fact that at first glance it cannot be decided, in respect of its significance in the broadest sense or even as an object of pleasure or pain in the special, i.e. the ethical sense. Is such otherness acceptable? I would say that it is unavoidable.'[9]

To defend the equal originality of the rights of the other despite the impossibility of deciding whether their intentions and effects are good or bad comes very close to the key determination of modern freedom of thought, unconditional acknowledgment. If that is the case, however, then postmodernity must also explore the implications of its advocacy of the right to differ – for example the universal norm of justice – and not dismiss it as oppressive.

> Without a consensual recognition of the key content of modern politics (human rights; democracy; the legal, constitutional, social state) – which embrace plurality, the existence of plurality cannot ultimately be assured. To this degree, that minimum of universal practical reason which Rawls claims in his theory of justice and Habermas in his theory of discourse seems simply indispensable.[10]

A further criterion for assessing an intellectual movement is to examine what ideas, measures and power of motivation it can offer in the face of social and individual aporias:

> The implications of this reduced practical reason for human rights and morals owe their plausibility and power of motivation, as Taylor shows, to particular ideological *sources*, the victory of which puts even this minimum in question. The postmodern insistence on the plurality of the heterogeneous accentuates this problem without contributing to its solution.[11]

III. Questions to the churches

The churches are also subject to the same criterion of the question of their resources for overcoming the conflicts of modernity, which have been substantially accentuated by the instrumental realization of reason in the form of power. How can they make it possible to experience the Christian message in the changed conditions of individualization and tendentious syncretistic *bric à brac*, the de-traditionalizing and de-doctrinalizing,[12] and introduce it into public decisions? Just as it is clear that two ways of mediation which were taken for granted, culture as a whole and the family, no longer support religious socialization as they used to, so too it is possible to recognize clearly the needs for orientation, meaning, belonging and comfort, meeting which is the task of the church in society. It can take up and encourage the desire to seek subjectively appropriate ways of relating to God and witnessing, instead of preventing it by its appearance and the forms of its communication and process of decision. The communitarian or even fundamentalist retreat into the enclaves of their own convictions and the refusal to collaborate and share responsibility in processes of counselling and legislation are not alternatives.

In his discussion of Kant's writings on religion, Paul Ricoeur goes above all into the middle of the three constitutive mediations of religion: 'representation, belief and the institution'.[13] The depiction of the principle of the good by the person of Jesus becomes effective in faith. Ricoeur sums up the content of the faith which is to be attested further in the combination of a modern and a postmodern term: 'selfness' and 'alterity', the 'alterity of help and the selfness of acceptance', the relationship between which he describes as 'paradoxical'(29). If the paradox of alterity and selfness, liberation and free assent, constitute the original experience of the biblical picture of human beings, which made an influential and decisive contribution with the rise of the consciousness of freedom in modernity; if, as we heard in Lyotard, insight into the incalculable value of the other is the basis of the respect for 'difference'; if this relationship of the self to alterity is 'postmodern', then long live postmodernity!

Translated by John Bowden

Notes

1. U. Barth, 'Schleiermachers Reden als religionstheoretisches Modernisierungs-programm', in S. Vietta and D. Kemper (eds), *Ästhetische Moderne in Europa. Grundzüge und Problemzusammenhänge seit der Romantik*, Munich 1998, 441–74: 452.

2. That growing into a linguistic community presupposes such original spontaneity not only rules out behaviourist theories about the first learning of language but also shows the one-sidedness of the fixation of the thinker obligated to the paradigm change from the philosophy of consciousness to the philosophy of language on the 'primacy of intersubjectivity' instead of taking the equal originality of both into account. For this problem, which is central to the understanding of freedom and the subject in modernity, the debate between D. Henrich and J. Habermas is crucial.

3. Cf. Dietrich Ritschl, 'Die christliche Kirche und die Vielfalt der Postmoderne', *Yonsei Journal of Theology* 2, 1997, 67–83: 75–77.

4. Hansjürgen Verweyen, Preface to Joachim Valentin, *Atheismus in der Spur Gottes. Theologie nach Jacques Derrida*, Mainz 1997, 8–13: 11.

5. Valentin, *Atheismus* (n.4), 18.

6. 'Thesen zur philosophischen Hermeneutik', *Internationale Zeitschrift für Philosophie* 1993, 173–88: 173 n.2, 174 n.4. For Krämer, the plurality of possibilities of exegesis populated by postmodernity does not mark any fundamental difference from modernity as long as it is not taken over into 'metaphysical statements like that of the equality in principle of all perspectives' (186). So in this respect he gives a negative answer to the question of the alternative of modernity and postmodernity: 'The accentuation of the hermeneutical pluralism in contemporary philosophy is welcome as a consequence of the de-Platonizing of modernity and as a corrective to

the tradition, but not as its alternative, which would only attract a counter-metaphysic that would be equally dogmatic . . . An expansion and completion of paradigms would thus be more welcome than a dramatic shift of perspective' (176).

7. Jügen Habermas, 'Die Einheit der Vernunft in der Vielfalt ihrer Stimmen', in id., *Nachmetaphysicsches Denken*, Frankfurt 1988, 153–86: 180.

8. Such a normative definition of modernity is lacking in Martin Henry's perceptive account of postmodern thinkers in 'God in Postmodernity', *Irish Theological Quarterly* 63, 1998, 3–21.

9. 'Die Ambivalenz des Fremden. J.-F. Lyotard im Gespräch', *Information Philosophie* 26, 1998, 28–33: 32f.

10. Arno Anzenbacher, *Christliche Sozialethik: Einführung und Prinzipien*, Paderborn 1997, 123.

11. Ibid., 122.

12. U. Barth finds the characteristic elements of Christian religion at the end of the twentieth century already anticipated 200 years previously (1799) in Schleiermacher's *Speeches*: 'All the characteristics mentioned – differentiation, de-dogmatizing, individualizing, pluralizing and de-institutionalizing – correspond quite closely to the elements which more recent sociology of religion has identified in the process of religious modernization. So it is no coincidence that this has had a positive relationship to Schleiermacher as one of its few theological precursors . . . The anchoring of the concept of the church in the structure of religious description and communication is aimed at the de-institutionalizing of the traditional pattern of organization of religious communities as public institutions of salvation in favour of social systems of symbolic communication' (Barth, 'Schleiermachers Reden' [n.1], 474).

13. *'la représentation, la croyance, et l'institution';* cf. Paul Ricoeur, 'Le destinataire de la religion: l'homme capable', in M. M. Olivette (ed.), 'Philosophie de la religion entre éthique et ontologie', *Archivio di Filosofia*, Padua 1998, 19–34: 29–31.

Christian Faith and Cultural Amnesia

Christian Duquoc

Despite the accumulation of commemorations, our era suffers from 'cultural amnesia', if I am to believe those who planned this issue. This statement leaves me perplexed. What is the basis for such a judgment? What investigation has led to it? Of what is there amnesia? Could the amnesia be of the twofold origin of Western culture: Greek and Judaeo-Christian? Or just the Judaeo-Christian tradition?

Suppose that the traditions which have modelled the West have been forgotten. A change in the relationship of our contemporaries to their past would confirm this. But to speak of amnesia would seem to me excessive, given the records on the monuments and in the literature which form our environment and remain there for us.

The cultural mutation

The contemporary mutation affects the relationship to former norms: traditions are no longer thought important as models; they are there to look at and investigate, but do not define either a possible way or a meaning. They relate to aesthetics, politics and ethics.

The traditions are there to be looked at or investigated by scholars. That is what is happening to the Christian tradition: its literary monument, the Bible, is studied; the art and architecture to which it has given rise is admired; it is no longer regarded as a source of truth, even if the works generally attributed to it provide aesthetic enjoyment. If there is amnesia, it is not cultural, but ethical, philosophical or religious. The Christian tradition is admired without being significant, for the referent to which it formerly related does not exist in society for the majority of our contemporaries. Thus in the case of Judaism and Christianity, the aesthetic value often remains present, but the philosophical or religious referent is thought uninteresting because it does not make sense.

The Greek tradition has not escaped this mutation, but here the mutation is less radical, since for a long time its referent had already been judged mythical. So the mutation relates essentially to the interrogative power of Greek philosophy. This is an element of investigation in scholarly debate; it occupies universities, but it no longer makes sense. If there is amnesia, it relates to the idea of truth: that no longer comes to us from a tradition. The past is not without interest, but it is without power. It is an object of commemoration, but no longer a vector of meaning.

If this brief analysis is along the right lines, the mutation in the relationship with the past relates essentially to truth and meaning: by reason of social evidence or a rumour, the traditions which brought the West into being are thought no longer to have any weight in the quest for the truth and the definition of meaning; they are objects of archaeology and are therefore interesting to the degree that learned investigations into our past arouse our curiosity. No future for our civilization will arise from these traditions; they are irrelevant. Have we to describe this phenomenon as amnesia? If we have, the amnesia would relate to the capacity to make sense of the traditions the works of which are available to us; it would not relate either to the content of culture or interest in literary and artistic monuments. This unprecedented and original perception of our past has an effect on faith and the way in which it is handed down, with the traditions forming to speak the background to what is available to believe.

Cultural complicity and faith

Until recently, in catechesis, ordinary preaching, teaching and the exchanges between generations, the Judaeo-Christian tradition in its many forms, ranging from the Bible to literary, pictorial and architectural developments of it, represented, even for non-believers, the common capital of Western civilization and to some degree the place of meaning *par excellence*. Popular faith depended on this generalized transmission. Even the anticlericalism reigning in nineteenth-century France did not attack this common root, since it did not stand apart from the moral principles and evaluation of customs of those figures who had grown up in the Judaeo-Christian tradition. Although Jules Ferry was anticlerical, he readily recognized this. Beyond question this is one of the reasons why the laity in France, committed to the teaching of a universal morality which had no link to any particular tradition, did not seem in any way to bring about a break in shared customs and convictions. The conflicts were all the stronger between Catholics and 'Republicans' because their thoughts and practices were close. The dissemination and explosion into contradictory practices only came about after the events of 1968. Until then, the Christian way of regarding practical life dominated life, even if it was not anchored in faith in the biblical God: it maintained a horizon of meaning.

The great social utopias which arose in the nineteenth century did not escape this complicity with Christianity: they had drawn a large part of their inspirations from its messianism and its prophecy on behalf of the poor. Their recent collapse, after their totalitarian and inhuman politics, has in the process damaged the Judaeo-Christian prophetic tradition, which had supported them in a clandestine way. The inability of these utopias to change the violent course of history and even more the increased horror that they brought has been highly detrimental to the idea that the Judaeo-Christian tradition held the key to meaning. If it has a value, it is aesthetic and can only indicate a meaning. The tradition, here especially the Judaeo-Christian tradition, has lost its secular authority. It is doomed to become a possible subject of investigation, of anecdote, of artistic or literary interest, but no longer has the value of a philosophical opinion inserted into the debate; it has only a monumental or an archaeological interest.

The still all too familiar character of this tradition and the feeling that it is irrelevant to the provision of any meaning in existence encourage amnesia. The tradition is too well known to be understood. Faith, trust in the transcendent God as the foundation of truth, now seems to be able to intrigue people or to raise questions only to the degree that it is detached from the cultural background which relegates it to a past that is now insignificant. If there were radical cultural amnesia, proclamation of this faith would come as a surprise. In reality, the current amnesia is not a forgetfulness but the result of a judgment: for many of our contemporaries, Christianity is simply an archaic monument like Gregorian music, Roman art or Greek architecture. It can be beautiful, but it is no longer true for us.

We are caught up in a paradox: a concern to snatch the monuments of Christianity from cultural oblivion is not necessarily a service to the transmission of faith; rather, it drives faith to be identified with what was, but which in our way of apprehending truth and meaning now risks being as irrelevant as a desire to write Gregorian music again or to construct buildings in a Romanesque style. By contrast, if there were real amnesia, i.e. a forgetfulness of what historical Christianity was in the works to which it gave rise or which it produced, it would be possible for an apparently new faith to reply to the questions which arise from the contradictions of our contemporary existence. To what point can this paradox be accepted?

Forgetfulness and faith

A comparison prompts a reflection which does not conform to the current pessimism that deplores the disappearance of culture. At the beginning of the sixteenth century in Valladolid there was a famous theological disputation between Bartolomeo de las Casas and a theologian named Sepulveda about the evangelization of the Indians. Sepulveda argued that it was unthinkable for the Indians to become Christians without adopting Spanish or Western culture, which was the almost natural vehicle of the biblical faith. Bartolomeo de las Casas held the opposite view, not only for the practical reasons of his cruel experience of the Spanish way of acculturating the Indians to Western customs, but on the principle that faith was sufficiently independent of any culture to have no need of an attachment to a culture for its content to become credible. The dispute did not produce a solution which convinced the opposite side.

All things being equal, our present situation of a break in the transmission of traditions which recently had a normative value that they have lost today is very like that with which the Christians of the Indian world were confronted: faith had to be proclaimed there without the support of a cultural vector. This situation led to the Westernization of the Indians, a Westernization which was largely defective.

To seek to act today as if the rehabilitation of a culture common to the West by reason of its origins were the prelude to a credible proclamation of the gospel would be tantamount to thinking that the link between our ancient form of civilization and Christian faith is so powerful that any break in continuity which does not arise from ecclesiastical policy would do considerable damage to faith. Can we accept that the link between the tradition which materialized in the West and faith is so evocative that forgetfulness of its significance would lead to not only a provisional devaluation of faith as a result of fashion, but structurally to a devaluation of faith itself? I doubt it.

The positive aspect of forgetfulness

Amnesia works in two ways: one which maltreats the values handed down at the heart of a civilization, the other which is an incentive to inventing new procedures so that the proclamation of the faith does not become the hostage of a social phenomenon.

The first effect has been discussed by educationalists. Disturbing phenomena, in particular delinquency and suicide among young people, raise questions about the failures in the transmission of values. The culture learned at school, college or university can provide learning, but it does not provide a meaning to life. Because of this it risks engendering rancour and bitterness towards those who are professionally responsible for handing down something that is devoid of relevance to everyday existence. It would be interesting to analyse the reasons for vandalism: it is directed against all forms which establish a certain order through values which are no longer recognized. These are felt to be aggression and not potential structures of the personality. What is called classical culture, and at least in France is the main element in scholarly education, does not in principle separate knowledge and the good life. That is also the case with science, despite the incantations of some humanist sages: knowledge is detaching itself radically from the good life and from happiness in life.

Knowledge which still has this concern is now thought of as archaic. The quest for the good life has led towards an explosion of instant enjoyment: the good life does not belong in the rational order; it relates to the irrational and the ephemeral. Classical culture, which mixed reason and the practice of co-existence, is now ineffective, since this form of reason is deprived of efficacy, not to mention viability. The amnesia is that of the value of a civilization which was the vehicle for this kind of culture which lost credibility because it was dominated by science, the cold and neutral form of reason. Discussions on education have a great future because it is not easy to find a social phenomena which evades good will.

The second effect, here understood within the sphere of Christian faith, is quite different: it relates to the capacity to innovate and to make sense of a faith which is not an accomplice of classical culture. Suppose we accepted the need to show the Christian faith, not as being in continuity with a shared ethic and with the Western tradition, but as arising from the most contemporary existential questions. The Bible belongs to a tradition only up to a certain point; in fact it is a living reality only if it is actualized in a community, i.e. confronted with the existential questions for which no reply has already been given, except by comparison with the questions which our predecessors asked themselves.

This hypothesis would perhaps allow us to envisage Christian faith no longer as the product of a culture which is only of aesthetic interest by reason of its archaic character, but as the other, which potentially damages all culture by reason of its refusal to integrate itself into the closure of meaning which is involved in every culture and the system of truth which each culture promotes. By virtue of this break, the Christian faith would cease to be a monument of the past and attain a status of existential relevance. This hypothesis calls for breaks with the tradition, which has often been institutionalized; it requires conversion by faith to the unexpected action of God. It is by no means the role of faith to take the place of a failing culture. Its role is not to save the institutions which are failing in the transmission of culture in a given civilization. It is by remaining itself at a distance that it indirectly reveals energy for all culture, particularly that in the West on which it left such a mark.

Translated by John Bowden

Fundamentalism, Integralism and Sects in the Church

Miklós Tomka

The title of this article contains a neutral statement of fact. Nevertheless, it is open to misunderstanding. In some ears it sounds like a battle-cry, or at least like the diagnosis of a dangerous epidemic. Implicitly one gets the impression that these phenomena are something new. At any rate, the phenomena themselves, fundamentalism, integralism and sectarianism, are regarded as a challenge. However, it seems to me that this view does not go deep enough. I shall be investigating it here. Given the relevance that the phenomena have, here in part I shall be examining their causes and in part their involvement in the church, in other words the way in which the church as the people of God and as an organization can and should live with these phenomena and the people who incorporate them.

In the past decade the theological and sociological literature on fundamentalism has reached vast proportions.[1] The concept, originally shaped in Protestant anti-modernism, has long since outgrown its cradle. With Islam and Hinduism it has entered the global scene. The media have discovered it as a topic.[2] Alongside religious fundamentalism we know and fear cultural and political fundamentalisms. The structural characteristics are the same: a fixation on a past situation (often more imagined than actually known), a self-understanding or interpretation of the world which is made absolute, which results in an ahistorical character and timelessness that is then utilized for understanding the present and the future. It is not the context but *the* truth itself which is to be knowable for ever, laid down in formal statements and unchangingly normative for all.[3]

In the Catholic sphere we have an additional variant, integralism. Oswald von Nell-Breuning calls this a religious totalitarianism.[4] Here the emphasis is less on timelessness than on a rejection of the autonomy of this-worldly realities. Integralism seeks to subject everything to religion and the religious – and to the direct power of the church.[5] Integralism shows the ongoing life of positions which were long since superseded in the Investiture Dispute, but which have been kept alive by the *de facto* cultural and political power of the church. Whereas fundamentalism shows itself to be predominantly ahistorical and absolutist, integralism attempts to undo or remove from sight the autonomy of society. The independent order would then come completely under the competence of religion and the church (of course the Catholic Church).

'Sects in the church' are cultural communities which set themselves apart from the whole of the tradition and the consensus (or the institutionalized positions) of the church by their constricted views and understandings of themselves (which are often, but not always, fundamentalist and/or integralist). The selection of and emphasis on what is believed, with its special content (which is arbitrary, but typical of the group), is safeguarded by demarcation from others, by exclusivity and elitism and by strong bonds of community. In this sense one can speak of 'structural heresies'.[6]

Epistemologically, all three phenomena may be said to suffer from a loss of totality (and thus of catholicity), simplification, formalism, a mechanistic and hierarchical structure of thought and a black-and-white polarization. These go hand in hand with a legalistic ethic. In terms of social structure, in modern society all three positions lead to segregation, to isolation, to the formation of ghettos, but often also to a lively internal culture with a marked sense of being 'us'. Among psychological motives mention is often made of a weak ego, anxiety about freedom and a fight from new developments and responsibility, which are typical phenomena of adolescence. The intensive practice of faith (though this is often formal and/or one-sided) and the often quite dogged intolerance are said to be compensations.

It is easy to list the main characteristics. But these seldom appear in a pure form. Opus Dei clearly seeks to bring about the kingdom of God with this-worldly means, through politics and power. The integralist feature is unmistakable. Archbishop LeFebvre's movement fulfils the criteria of fundamentalism in every respect. There are also other manifestly fundamentalist groups which have arisen out of a rejection of developments after the Council. But a clear programme is more the exception. So there can be difficulties in making straightforward classifications. Which of the more recent religious groups and revivalist movements are the 'hopes of the universal church'[7] and which are fundamentalists, integralists and sects within the church. Occasionally Communione e Liberazione, the Focolare Movement, the Catholic charismatic movement or even all new spiritual movements are condemned root and branch as fundamentalisms. Is their programme fundamentalist? Or their mentality? Or are their members fundamentalists? And if it is the members, are the fundamentalists in the majority, or the loudest, or the new converts? For a while great enthusiasm can prove blinding and alienate others, but that is far from being fundamentalist. On the contrary, the discriminatory war-cry 'Fundamentalists!' can resound from a similarly narrow-minded perspective.[8] The refusal to accept a religious differentiation within the church corresponding to the varieties of societies and cultures can be just as fundamentalist as nailing oneself to certain tenets of faith or modes of behaviour.

The historical location of the three phenomena mentioned produces a strange contradiction. Clearly there have always been fundamentalist hardenings, integralist positions and sectarian segregations in the church. For a time they were powerful or even dominant. But one gets the impression that in the modern world these have taken on a new quality, or a new status within the church. They are interpreted as expressions of modernity or reactions against it. If this assessment is to some degree correct, the context is also of decisive importance.

Here modernity will be described, quite briefly, as the structural fragmentation of society, as an increase in complexity and contingency, as a loss of the social mediation of unity and patterns of thought which can be taken for granted. The autonomy of various spheres of life and the increase and differentiation of the roles of individuals lead to an increase in individual freedoms but also to a continual need to choose between the alternatives offered, or to the possibility, or even unavoidability, of an independent shaping of identity. Over wide areas, prior shaping by society is giving way to individualization. The extent and influence of social institutions is declining; they are being relativized.

The establishment of modernity also affects religion and the church. The general trend is towards a growing degree of (a) religion distanced from the church, (b) religion detached from patterns handed down by the church, or also (c) a decline in any form of religion. There are changes even within the church community. The fact of the social and cultural multiplicity of the people who make up the church is a challenge to its unity. The existential and emotional dimensions of daily life exert pressure towards revaluing religion as a supplement to a cognitive rationality and a legal order which has become impersonal. But these dimensions can hardly be institutionalized; or the possibilities for institutionalizing them have yet to be explored. At any rate, individual interpretation and personal implementation are becoming increasingly significant as compared with existing institutions. That gives rise to a new situation of being the church which more than ever before reflects that actual differences between believers.

On the basis of an optimism about modernization one can easily come to a false conclusion about fundamentalism. A number of people conjure up the dream of Christianity really being the religion of 'adult Christians'. By this they mean mature, modern individuals, capable both of defining their Christianity for themselves and also successfully finding their way through, and establishing themselves in, a changing and complex environment. These individuals are said to be able to cope with the complexity of conditions, to be ready for exchanges, and always prepared for dialogue with those who think otherwise. Accordingly the future is said to belong to those Christians who have rejected any fundamentalist and integralist hardening and sectarianism. According to this classification, the last-mentioned phenomena are merely expressions of social or psychological retardation. Some groups are said not to be able to cope with modernity because they have come on the scene late. Others are marginalized in social and economic terms and therefore do not have the capacity to assert their position in a changing and pluralistic environment. Yet others are simply said not to be sufficiently socialized. They have not experienced the security needed for the formation of a stable identity. An insufficient religious socialization can also be assumed. Those who have been brought up to see religion as having an instrumental function or to a Christianity administered by the clergy find it difficult to struggle through to a personal religious autonomy. In all instances, however, these are the problems sometimes of remnants, sometimes of deviants, the treatment of whom belongs not so much in normal life as in a form of social healing.

However, the question is whether the above views do justice to modernity. The basic characteristics of modernity in fact include the increasing complexity and unprecedented acceleration of change. These mean a further decline in the power of the communal and institutional safeguards of human forms of life (including the family), excessive demands on individuals in shaping their identity while at the same time being isolated and increasingly burdened. Modernity makes it necessary for individuals to find their identity when increasingly social relationships and models for action which previously helped to create identity are being removed. Thus modernity is 'producing' people who, unable to cope, cannot define their identity in the all-embracing yet changing context of society and culture or secure a place in an ever-extending social environment, and therefore define a place for themselves in their particularity, in individual sectors of culture and society, in smaller groups, in already existing inherited patterns, in the private sphere.

Whether such people are to be regarded as the 'norm' or simply as the great majority of modern society need not be discussed here. What is important for our reflections, though, is the fact that in former times the formation of identity (though mediated through small communities) was more institutionalized and supported than it is today along the lines of an order accepted throughout society or by models laid down by the whole church. In other words, it was more uniform. Central cultural control was much more powerful. By contrast, in the modern world there are marked divergences. Identity is increasingly formed by individual effort and in the context of unique circumstances, situations and groups. However, the special relationships are mostly fragmentary. A diminution of totality stands in another dimension over against individualization and the possibility of personalization. This is a process in which the use of terms like 'normality' and maturity or retardation or 'deviation' seem out of place; they can all too easily be expressions of an ideologized, or pre-modern framework of reference.

Some sociological analyses of fundamentalism compare it with child-hood immaturity. The naivety, the immediacy, the devotion to be found in it can be classified as childlike, as can the undifferentiated perspective, the lack of an over-view and the resultant tendency towards error, or the irritation with deviant views and the inability to cope with more complex situations. However, Jesus made noteworthy statements about children and their faith . . .

On a basic level one cannot avoid attacking fundamentalism, integral-ism and sectarianism (even within the church) as curtailments of Christianity, as limitations on the freedom which God offers us, as structural sins. Nor can this obligation be reduced by the conviction that in the fundamentalist (etc.) movements and groups there is much unselfishness and a great deal of the true nature of the church (even if it is used wrongly).

On a pragmatic, ecclesiological level, one must note these tendencies as religious expressions of a variety of cultural fixations and tension. They represent inadequacies or hurts, but those involved in them by no means lose their right to religious articulation as a result. In this perspective, fundamentalists, integralists and even their possibly sectarian groups also have a right to existence in the church, though conversely one of the central tasks of communion is to reconcile the intolerant and irreconcil-able, to heal the wounded and loosen up fixations which result in a deprivation of freedom.

On a human level, the starting point must be that the cause of fundamentalisms, integralisms and sects does not usually lie in the theoretical but in the sphere of human relationships: in a lack of love in childhood, in disruptions to interpersonal relations, in the experience of not being accepted, in human isolation, in an unfulfilled need for love. Here arguments do not help. On the contrary. A crystal-clear proof can only humiliate those who think otherwise and confirm to them once again that one goes by principles instead of accepting real people. Here what is needed is a quiet acceptance of the other which shows that one values his or her person rather than dialogue (or even a discussion); love as a Christian duty independent of ideology.[9]

This short survey must end here. But a postscript is necessary. The church is not only the mystical body of Christ and communion and the people of God on the way, but also an institution in the strait-jacket of an all-too-this-worldly bureaucracy. The communion can sympathetically endure petrifications of individual parts, especially if it tries to revive and free them. But the bureaucratic structure has a structural affinity to fundamentalism and integralisms. These lack independence and are subservient to authority. They seek to eternalize the customary and oppose innovations. In this way they try to strengthen the church. They are predictable. They are mere shadows of themselves and have to treasure administration. To avoid any misunderstanding: of course the church is not simply a bureaucracy. But it also has an organization which cannot avoid following the rules of bureaucracies and the apparatus of power here and now. These are the very places in which fundamentalisms and integralisms can expect partnership and support. However, the relationships which come into being in this way can go on to pave the way for revaluations of church law or premature beatifications of founders. They can give the impression that the ministry of the church affirms fundamentalisms. As so often, here too the institutional can work against the spirit of liberation.

Translated by John Bowden

Notes

1. Cf. Norman J. Cohen (ed.), *The Fundamentalist Phenomenon*, Grand Rapids 1990; Bruce B. Lawrence, *Defenders of God*, San Francisco 1989; Martin E. Marty and R. Scott Appleby (eds), *Fundamentalisms Observed*, Chicago 1991, and further volumes of The Fundamentalism Project.

2. Gilles Kepel, *La Revanche de Dieu. Chrétiens, juifs et musulmans à la reconquête du monde*, Paris 1991.

3. Paul Ladrière and René Luneau (eds), *Le retour des certitudes. Événements et orthodoxie depuis Vatican II*, Paris 1987.

4. Oswald van Nell-Breuning, 'Integralismus', *Lexikon für Theologie und Kirche* 5, Freiburg 1960, 718.

5. Cf. also Karl Rahner, 'Theological Reflections on the Problem of Secularization', *Theological Investigations* 10, London and New York 1973, 318–48.

6. Wolfgang Beinert, 'Der katholische Fundamentalismus und die Freiheitbotschaft der Kirche', in id. (ed.), *Katholischer Fundamentalismus. Häretische Gruppen in der Kirche?*, Regensburg 1991, 52–89.

7. Thus in the encyclical *Evangelii nuntiandi* of Pope Paul VI.

8. Marty and Appleby even feel that endorsement of the dogma of the virgin birth and traditional belief in the physical resurrection of Christ is dangerous fundamentalism. Cf. Martin E. Marty and A. Scott Appleby, *The Glory and the Power. The Fundamentalist Challenge to the Modern World*, Boston 1992.

9. Hermann Denz and Paul M. Zulehner, 'Fundamentalismus: eine Herausforderung für die Alltagspraxis der Kirche', in Hermann Kochanek (ed.), *Die verdrängte Freiheit. Fundamentalismus in den Kirchen*, Freiburg 1991.

Aesthetic Culture as a Secular Religion?

Karl-Josef Kuschel

Anyone reflecting today on the relationship between aesthetics and religion cannot avoid noting that the church lost two classical, traditional models of this relationship.[1] Both models have once again found their way into the texts of the Second Vatican Council.

I. Traditional models of association worn out

In a well-meaning way, the Catholic Church believed that it had to say yet another word about the relationship between the church and art in its Constitution on the Sacred Liturgy. Even if the reference here was primarily to 'sacred art', it became clear how little even at that time these statements, metaphors and all, applied to the concrete situation of the artist:

> For that reason holy Mother Church has always been the patron of the fine arts and has ever sought their noble ministry, to the end especially that all things set apart for use in divine worship should be worthy, becoming, and beautiful, signs and symbols of things supernatural. And to this end she has trained artists. In fact the Church has, with good reason, always claimed the right to pass judgment on the arts, deciding which of the works of artists are in accordance with faith, piety, and the laws religiously handed down, and are to be considered suitable for sacred use. The Church has been particularly careful to see that sacred furnishings should worthily and beautifully serve the dignity of worship. She has admitted changes in material, style, or ornamentation prompted by the progress of technical arts with the passage of time (no. 122).

The church indeed meant well when it once again recalled its history and function in encouraging art. And who would dispute the fact that time and again the church has inspired, legitimated and financed art? In history the church was always also a factor which shaped culture and produced art. But do these statements still fit the present-day situation, even among artists who grapple with religious themes? 'Noble ministry', 'trained artists', the church is arbiter? No, that was all well meant, but the well meant, as we know, is the opposite of the good.

A second model of the relationship between the church and art is expressed in the Pastoral Constitution on 'The Church in the Modern World'. There we read:

> In their own way literature and art are very important in the life of the Church. They seek to give expression to man's nature, his problems and his experience in an effort to discover and perfect man himself and the world in which he lives; they try to discover his place in history, and in the universe, to throw light on his suffering and his joy, his needs and his potentialities, and to outline a happier destiny in store for him. Hence they can elevate human life, which they express under many forms according to various times and places (no.62).

This too was well meant. For here the church attaches 'great significance' to art. This is expressed above all in the function of art in providing a diagnosis of the time. Men and women discover themselves in the mirror of art, and this self-knowledge is used practically for the preaching of the church. The only problem is that such a 'utilization' of art is deeply ambivalent. On the one hand it is an expression of an unavoidable need for art, but at the same time it is also the expression of a secondary functionalization. Here the church side employs a convenient model of work-sharing. The artists make 'efforts' to understand the peculiar nature of human beings; taking on from here, the church produces the truth about this nature. The positions of the writers are allowed as 'unanswered questions', as indications, traces, beginnings; afterwards church doctrine brings the fragmentary to full knowledge. Here the claim of art to autonomy is overlooked, as are the questions that can be raised about the church's anthropology. With this model of work-sharing the church can remain unchanged. The relationship between art and the church is understood as one of question and answer.

II. The aestheticizing of the present-day world

All experts on the scene realize that there is need for a radical new definition of the relationship between religious and aesthetic culture. This is not only because the church and its theology have largely become irrelevant for the autonomous sphere of art. Wieland Schmied once summed up this irrelevance, which has often been remarked on and demonstrated, on the occasion of a pioneering exhibition of contemporary art in Berlin in 1990:

> *God is dead* – in the church. The churches seem to be godforsaken. So let us made a wide detour round them, *for God's sake*. God is no longer at home in the church. So let us look for him where perhaps we can still find him: in the remnants of the nature that is left to us; in the thickets of the cities, in the eyes of someone who looks at us; in the works of art.[2]

However, the present situation has changed once again, in that aesthetic culture itself has achieved the status of a religion: a secular religion, paradoxical though that may seem. By religion here is meant above all a 'status' which is given to aesthetic culture. There is no mistaking the fact that the aestheticizing of the world in which we live, above all in the countries shaped by industrialization, has made unstoppable progress. Through the media of image and print, every day not only do millions of people have reality prepared for them aesthetically, but viewers and readers necessarily develop an aesthetic sense about the world which is prepared for them in this way. The products of the history of art, older and more recent, make more and more people sensitive and give them orientation.

In practice, it works like this. Whereas the museums – especially with special exhibitions – attract an international public of millions, all the old institutions which provided orientation, like the churches, are increasingly losing significance. Those who diagnose our culture speak with some justification of our culture being turned into a museum. In so doing they confirm the long-cherished expectation that in a post-Christian world, for millions of people the museums have replaced the churches; the artists the priests; the objects the altars. Theatre and film premières are often still regarded as the only 'events' which can transcend a banal everyday reality. Like religious pilgrims, tourists interested in art seek the physical proximity of the objects they revere; like pilgrims, they often take home souvenirs which preserve the memory of the 'holy' place. The autonomous work of art has taken the place of the cultic image, and the sights and places associated with the great masters have taken the place of relics and the tombs of the saints. What other explanation is there of this than that the places where famous artists were born and lived, indeed even where they died and were buried, have become tourist attractions of the first order?

Moreover sociologists of culture like Gerhard Schulze describe our reality as an 'experience society' and speak of an 'aestheticizing of everyday life' which has been taking place in various phases since the end of the Second World War. What they mean by this is that whereas in the post-war period up to 1968 many families in Germany and comparable European countries were concerned above all with survival, and the modest offers of experience (the cinema, theatre, concerts, radio) provided 'were experienced against the dark background of complete deprivation', today millions of people no longer just survive but experience. After modest beginnings in the post-war period, the 1960s were marked by a first 'enormous phase of aestheticizing'. Equipped with ever-increasing potential in the quest for experience (time, money, mobility, equipment), consumers discovered that the whole of everyday life could be aestheticized. In other words, the public seized on unlimited listening to music, travelling, buying clothes, eating and drinking, sex, dancing and going out in the evenings. And this wealth of experience developed even more hectically in the 1980s. Western European societies turned completely into experience societies in which a market of experiences did not satisfy real needs but dependencies which people had themselves created. According to Schulze, in the 1980s:

The experience market developed into the dominant sphere of daily life. It marshalled enormous resources in the capacity for production, the potential for enquiry, political energy, intellectual activity and living time. For a long time the public and those offering experience have been played off against each other. In a routine way the producers utilize the unwritten rules of the marketing of experience, increasingly resorting to techniques of suggestion. The experience market is still a growth area. Alongside the growth path of expansion (the expansion of the range of production, the expansion of the sales of given types of product, and the expansion of sales areas), the growth path of intensification has been taken (the intensification of depth of experience, refinement, and the heightening of quality).[3]

Thus it is almost a sign of helplessness when even in official texts of the German Conference of Bishops the lack of cultural and aesthetic competence is now being noted, and in the training of priests and theologians education in aesthetic competence is being called for. However, one thing should be noted as the sign of an intensification of awareness. Though so far unfortunately it is no more than an announcement, here at least the intention should be emphasized and its concrete implementation should be urged:

The arts should be integral elements in the study of theology. That applies in particular to graphic art, architecture, literature and music,

which have tremendous significance in the tradition and life of the church. Theologians, catechists and teachers of religion must be put in a position to deal responsibly with artistic questions and decisions. Here practice and study is needed in the following fields:
– Discussion of the lines of developement in the history of the various arts;
– Insight into current conceptions and questions and their origin;
– Grappling with the foundations of the history of art, and with philosophy and aesthetics;
– An intensification of the capacity for perception; the development of a sense of the methodological problems bound up with this;
– Investigations of the various settings of the arts in the life of the church and theology and the specific conditions for their reception.[4]

III. Against aestheticizing as a substitute religion

Thus two things are bound up with cultural competence: gaining knowledge and at the same time a capacity for criticism; gaining experience and criteria for 'discerning the spirits'. A false aestheticizing of religion or a false sacralization of secular culture is to be resisted.

For if aestheticizing becomes a substitute religion, the perception or shaping of the world becomes a matter of personal taste, purely arbitrary and random. Whatever gives pleasure is allowed. And where that happens, communities risk losing their inner links. Old alloys crumble. A society develops in which a culture of experience seems to establish itself at the expense of a culture of ideals. Greed for private amusement is increasingly satisfied at the cost of the common good; ever more refined offers from the experience industry establish themselves at the expense of a lowering of the threshold of shame. In short, in a society in which aesthetic culture becomes a secular religion, unnoticed by many there has been a great shift: standards of living and enjoyment of life are already regarded as the meaning of life.

In this situation, an article by probably the most famous dramatist of German literature in our day, Botho Strauss, came as a shock to many people. In 1993 *Der Spiegel* published an essay of his, and rarely have the remarks of a writer on the situation of the time provoked such a polarized reaction.[5] A few passages must suffice here:

Thesis 1: We Western Europeans have lived 'morally above our means'. We have allowed all values to be mocked.

A hyper-critical public morality which at any time tolerated (when it did not practise) contempt for Eros, contempt for the soldier, contempt for the church, tradition and authority. It is not surprising that its words no longer have any importance in emergencies. But in whose hand, in whose mouth, is the power and the eloquence to avert worse?

Thesis 2: At some point there will be 'a violent explosion against the deception of the senses'. This deception takes place in the 'electronic commercialism' which presents the world to its public in the most illusory ways possible.

> The regime of the telecratic public is the most unbloody of violent rules and at the same time the most comprehensive totalitarianism in history. It does not need to make any heads roll; it makes them superfluous. It knows no subjects and no enemies. It knows only collaborators, those who conform to the system. Consequently people no longer notice that the power of agreement misuses them, exploits them, mutilates them to the point where they are not recognizably human.

What is Strauss's alternative to this? A 'far-reaching change of mentality born from the danger', a 'final farewell to a concept of culture, hostile to devotion, which has now lasted for a century and which, in the footsteps of Nietzsche, has overpopulated our spiritual and cultural living space with countless mockers, atheists and frivolous insurgents, creating its own bigoted piety of the political, the critical and the anything-can-be-criticized'. Here Strauss's imagination does not paint 'a future world empire'; it does not need a political utopia, but seeks to rejoin 'the length of days, the unmoved.' It aims at 'in-depth remembrance' and 'to this degree is a religious or proto-political initiation'. It is always and existentially a 'fantasy of loss and not of the (earthly) promise. So it is a fantasy of the poet, from Homer to Hölderlin.'

Strauss's analyses and counter-moves will have to be weighed up carefully in the sphere of theology and ethics – by grappling with his plays and his essays, through which, from his 'Trilogy of Reunion', 'Great and Small' and 'Couples, Passers-By' to a collection of aphorisms like 'No Beginning. Reflections on Spot and Line' (1992), a quest runs for the presence or absence of the divine and a trace of theological and ethical reflection. All these quests, shaped in a highly artificial, formal aesthetic mastery in the plays, and all the often aphoristically brief reflections, have a *fundamentum in re*: they resist the reality of the problem of nihilism in the sphere of art.

In fact Strauss the dramatist is beyond question one of those intellectuals in Germany who have detected that the crisis in aesthetics cannot be discussed and diagnosed in depth unless a new discussion is opened up about ethics and aesthetics, art and truth, focussed on the theme of the problem of nihilism. Critics have rightly observed that: 'Under the sign of postmodernity, that time seems to be dawning which Nietzsche proudly prophesied in isolation more then a century ago.'[6] In my view, we also have to bid farewell to a 'concept of culture which is hostile to devotion', which in the footsteps of Nietzsche has populated the cultural and intellectual sphere in which we live with countless mockers, and created its own bigoted piety of the critical and the anything-can-be-criticized. Here we need to remember a remark by Thomas Mann, with which he bade farewell to a Nietzschean atheism after the Second World War:

> We have come to know it (evil) in all its wretchedness and are no longer aesthetes enough to be afraid of the confession of good and to be ashamed of such trivial concepts and models as truth, freedom, justice . . . An aesthetic world view is simply incapable of dealing with the problems which we are obliged to resolve.[7]

And here we must add that an aesthetic culture which has become a secular religion is worth putting below 'Feuerbach' among the instruments of the modern critique of religion.

Translated by John Bowden

Notes

1. For these problems see K. J. Kuschel, *Im Spiegel der Dichter. Mensch, Gott und Jesus in der Literatur des 20. Jahrhunderts*, Düsseldorf 1997.

2. W. Schmied, *Gegenwärtigkeit. Spuren des Transzendenten in der Kunst unserer Zeit*, Stuttgart 1990, 21.

3. C. Schulze, *Die Erlebnisgesellschaft. Kultursoziologie der Gegenwart*, Frankfurt am Main and New York 1993, 542.

4. The German Catholic Bishops' Conference on Art and Culture in Theological Training, 5 October 1993.

5. B. Strauss, 'Anschwellender Bocksgesang', in *Der Spiegel* 6/1993, 202–7. A longer version of this text is published in *Der Pfahl. Jahrbuch aus dem Niemandsland zwischen Kunst und Wissenschaft* VII, Munich 1993, 9–25.

6. J. Früchtl, 'Ethik und Ästhetik. Eine nachmetaphysische Attraktion', *Philosophische Rundschau* 39, 1992, 2–28: 13. This judgment is based on the extensive investigation by B. Reuber, *Ästhetische Lebensformen bei Nietzsche*, Munich 1988.

7. T. Mann, 'Nietzsches Philosophie im Lichte unserer Erfahrung', in id., *Leiden und Grosse der Meister*, Frankfurt am Main 1982, 838–75: 873f.

Part III · Prospect

Should We Strive for a New Council?

Christoph Theobald and Dietmar Mieth

Nowadays this question is often asked, probably also because there is a growing awareness in the church that a series of problems raised in this issue need to be worked out openly. To resolve them is far beyond the capacities of any individuals – even though the individual may be Peter's successor or his advisers. People then reflect on the well-tried synodical structures of the church which have been revived at all levels since Vatican II and in the last thirty years have issued in a series of continental synods, of which a Third Vatican Council could be the crown. Though there is also a danger that here the church and the gospel could be confused with the staging of great mass scenes or a complicated authority for solving problems, legally regulated and bureaucratically administered, this option for a new council cannot be left out of account.

1. First of all we need to attempt to give a theological interpretation of the period in which we stand, the turning point of an era, especially as an 'extraordinary' event like a council has always been and should remain a response to a special *kairos* of the coming of God into his world which is experienced on all sides.

Now the four concluding articles of this issue make it clear how much the cultural and spiritual situation of humankind has changed since Vatican II; this also means that we cannot understand ourselves exclusively today in terms of the process of the reception of the last Council, whether this has now been successfully brought to a conclusion or whether it remains controversial. But what then, in the sense of the questions raised in this issue, is the really new element in our situation?

'Globalization' and the encounters which it brings, involving conflict to a greater or lesser degree, intercultural and intercontinental, both inside and outside the church, call for a global – 'ecumenical' – reinterpretation of the gospel. This hermeneutical task, which Christian awareness has never put to itself in such a way before, relates to all spheres of human life, down to relations between men and women, which touch on the deepest sources of life. Certainly this process of a global *aggiornamento* can refer back to traditions in a critical reception of the 'signs of the time'. But the 'exodus' of Christianity from its Mediterranean home (cf. Collet's article) also affects its normative state, or what is generally regarded as its normative state. That raises the question of truth and, indissolubly connected with it, the question of the communicative discovery of the truth. These questions are raised correctly in theology today only if it becomes clear that the divine revelation in history is completely and utterly in the hands of our creative processes of reception, which are fraught with risk. Because revelation is plural (four Gospels, a plurality of particular churches, and so on), it can remain present only in encounters made in the experience of faith and by way of a shared discovery of the truth. That is the case precisely because we are promised that revelation will abide in history to the end and here gives individuals who are called (for example Peter and his faith) a prophetic position which can never be dissolved into majority decisions.

2. The problematical character of this claim has become increasingly clear since the last Council under the pressure of our cultural and religious pluralism and of the immense task which is bound up with it, even if great theological and structural resistance reigns. Perhaps in this situation of 'transition' we might reflect that John XXIII did not link his notion of a council directly to traditional models. In referring time and again, to the end, to the vision of Pentecost and also to Luke's idea of a council, he wanted to stress the spiritual openness and unpredictability of the situation which he had created, and by his silence to enable the debates to be as free as possible. Thus, as Alberigo has pointed out, the first period of the Council, which did not approve a single text, remains the paradigm of a free quest for truth and conciliar dealings.

A series of articles distributed through the middle part of this issue (moral theology, church reform, etc.) make it clear that the matter is not one of working on problems of *content*; it relates rather to *forms* of dealing with one another and the shared search for truth. There is increasingly a general awareness that while the quest for answers and solutions in fundamental spheres of our life calls for rational discourse, it must also resort to a great variety of experiences. Thus, as individual French bishops have recently put it, the church needs to understand itself as a laboratory, a workshop or a field of experiments in which all have a say; humane forms of procedure are cultivated; and above all each individual, group and particular church is allowed to advance or to change its time. This could well be the meaning of the concept of a general church conciliarity. For the first time in history, Vatican II presented all the faithful with the four Gospels, each in its distinctive form, for liturgical reading. Will the forms of encounter depicted here be able to set in motion our past forms of culture, which have grown up in history, and church and social structures which have often been legalistically petrified?

3. Thus, lastly, the decisive open question is how the Gospels can show themselves historically to be an effective word of God and not just, as often in tradition, material for private devotion, or be left to the ideal of perfection in individual church religious societies or groups. The theological articles in the first part of this issue are all dominated by this concern. Has not the twentieth century led to an incredible revolution in the image of God? Whereas since the Fourth Lateran Council the European consciousness has been driven by the 'ever greater dissimilarity of God', today we are asking about the 'ever greater humanity of God' and God's way of dealing with our inhumanity. That affects not only the credibility of God but also that of all his witnesses to its foundations. Are their forms of life and action and also the institutional forms of their cohesion as a church a historical realization of the humanity of God which they proclaim? Do they point to God's 'ever greater humanity'? Certainly 'the tone makes the music' and it is important for the impatient patience of the gospel also to be heard in this question.

Should we expect a new Council? A church assembly which limited itself to continuing the promulgation of a series of compromises is always possible, and perhaps also necessary. However, only if it faced the radical nature of the question posed above would it do justice to its ecumenical calling. The question is whether the *kairos* has come for this and whether we grasp it.

Translated by John Bowden

Documentation: The Future of Particular Churches

José Oscar Beozzo

The subject of the 'particular church' (see note 3) has a crucial place on the list of questions concerning the future of the Christian faith. The question is not just an internal matter of how to conceive and organize relations between particular churches and the church of Rome, but above all a way of responding creatively and courageously to local challenges in the areas of economics, society, politics, culture and religion.

Also at stake are the relationship of the church with the world and how it can serve the poorest, the exercise of internal collegiality, and the co-responsibility of everyone in evangelization. Equally important are the questions of the local church's credibility in ecumenical dialogue and the quest for a reconciled unity in which its originality and historical identity can be welcomed and not despised and suppressed. The question of the future of particular churches within the Catholic Church, one of the major novelties of the post-Vatican II period, is taking on a new urgency by virtue of the debate on ecclesiological models and the dynamic of ecumenical relationships.

The extreme centralization that followed the Council of Trent and was accentuated after Vatican I means that treaties of ecclesiology begin their theses with the Roman Pontiff and the universal church, without ever reaching the local church gathered around its bishop as the real place where the church 'happens' and in which people are bound together by a living community, into which they come through baptism and confirmation and in which they grow through celebration of the word and the eucharist and reception of the other sacraments, through taking part in evangelization, catechesis and works of charity on behalf of justice and the poor.

Vatican II reinstated the particular or local church gathered around its bishop as the basis of ecclesiology, the place where the universal church, woven out of the threads binding the communion of churches together and to the see of Rome is incarnated and made into whole cloth (*Lumen Gentium* 26ff.).

New ways of being church

Anyone approaching Riobamba in Ecuador along the roads beaten by the cold winds of the Andean high plateau will be struck by the imposing bulk of Mt Chimborazo, with its glaciers gleaming white in the sun shining on its 19,500 foot summit. They will be equally struck by the harshness of that bare landscape, contrasting with the glowing colours of the indigenous products used to produce the women's clothing, the heritage of an ancient tradition going back over more than 7,000 years of history. The material poverty of the villages contrasts strongly with the cultural richness of the Andean civilization and now with the people's consciousness of their recovered dignity. In the communities, the local Indian leaders lead the celebration, proclaiming the word of God from the Bible no longer in Spanish but in a translation into Quechua, the life-long dream of the bishop from 1954 to 1985, Mgr Leónidas Proaño (1910–88),[1] who shared out the church's lands among the local inhabitants, trained catechists and sent them into every mountain valley, and founded a Centre for Indigenous Formation for the leaders of these communities. The purpose of his diocese was 'to build the church of the poor in the poor and from the poor, to make it a community, people of God, an expressive sign of the Kingdom of God on earth'.[2] Ten years after his death the memory of this father of the local church of Riobamba remains alive. One of his native catechists, Delfín Tenezaca, is today episcopal co-vicar for pastoral care of the indigenous peoples and another, Maximiliano Asadovay, is director of the Santa Cruz Centre for Indigenous Formation.

In Sao Luís do Maranhao in Brazil, on 19 July 1997, around 30,000 people filled the Maria Aragao square, while the sun set over the sea and the moon rose over the altar, to celebrate the closing eucharist of the Ninth Interchurch Meeting of Brazilian basic ecclesial communities (CEBs), whose motto was 'CEBs. Life and Hope of the Masses'. Community delegates from 240 of the country's 256 dioceses, after five years of intense preparation, together with sixty bishops, some hundred Protestants from other churches, delegates from the CEBs of other Latin American and Caribbean countries, and visiting theologians, bishops and journalists from Europe, the United States and Canada, had come together in a sort of great council of the church of the poor. The opening ceremony, held five days earlier in the same square, traced the course of the local black culture, of its religious expression in songs and the dances of the 'Bumba meu Boi' group; the strong women's presence was notable, and a welcome was given to representatives of over thirty indigenous Brazilian peoples, each with their different ways of celebrating and praising God (see the report in *The Tablet*, 2 August 1997, 996).

From 12 to 28 October 1992 the Fourth General Conference of Latin American Bishops was held in Santo Domingo, inaugurated with an address by Pope John Paul II and enshrined in a document setting out the conclusions reached by the bishops gathered there, who were accompanied by priests, men and women religious, lay women and men, theologians and Protestant observers.

From 16 November to 12 December 1997, in the wake of various continental synods (Africa, Europe and then Asia and Oceania), the Synod for America met in Rome, with 297 participants from all the countries of South, Central and North America and the Caribbean: bishops, theologians, lay people and invitees from other Christian churches.

What do these four events have in common?

In the first place, none of them would have been thinkable forty years earlier, when John XXIII began his pontificate following the death of Pius XII: the liturgy was in Latin and celebrated uniformly throughout the church; concentration of power in the hands of the pope, in the wake of Vatican I and the definition of papal infallibility, was such that some theologians held that it would never be necessary to convene another council; and Catholic ecumenism was summed up in the call to 'separated brethren' to renounce their errors and return to the one fold of Christ's flock.

In the second place, all these events represent ecclesial expressions born of Vatican II, involving the participation, on various levels, of the whole people of God in the life of the church. One can see these expressions in the distinctive face of the local church of Riobamba, inculturated in the Quechua world;[3] in the massive popular gathering of the base communities of another local church, that of Brazil, in which a significant number of its bishops took part; at the Interchurch Meeting in Sao Luis; and in the two different ways of expressing episcopal collegiality, the general conferences of the Latin American bishops and the Roman synods. And all include particular attention to the ecumenical dimension, to inter-religious and inter-cultural dialogue, and to the church's responsibilities for defending human rights and promoting justice and peace.

The question that hangs in the air is: what is the future for these new diversified and inculturated ways of being church; for the active participation of the baptized of both sexes in a great variety of services and ministries; for the quest for corresponding community through co-ordinating the basic communities, through pastoral, parish, diocesan and national councils; for the exercise of collegiality in bishops' conferences and synods; for the rise of new bodies dedicated to ecumenism and inter-religious dialogue?

The first answer is that these forms of being church have gained strength and generated initiatives that are spreading and consolidating themselves through the four quarters of the world, winning solid pastoral and theological support and becoming part of everyday life and church vocabulary.

The century of the laity

None of this would be possible without a basic movement that has changed the face of Catholicism: the twentieth century, called the century of the laity, has witnessed a gradual declericalization of many aspects of church life. Mission has come to be seen as a task for all the baptized; in the social sphere, the struggle for justice and human advancement have been adopted as essential dimensions of faith in relation to the world; the liturgical movement has led to the active participation of lay people in the liturgical assembly; the Bible has moved out of the hands of specialists into daily use in the simplest communities where men and – even more – women and young people have taken on a multiplicity of new ministries; ecumenical consciousness and practice have brought churches and faiths together in shared prayer, services and initiatives.

Another notable change has been the geographical shift in the demography of the Catholic and Reformed Churches: while Rome, Geneva and Canterbury are still the reference points for Roman Catholicism, the World Council of Churches and the Anglican Communion respectively, the majority of their faithful are found no longer in Europe but in the southern hemisphere, faced with the dramatic problems of hunger, poverty, illiteracy, epidemics and exclusion from the global market in work and consumption. These faithful from the periphery have brought their churches a new vigour in Christian life, a witness to the struggle for justice persevering to the point of martyrdom, a movement of incarnation in thousands of different cultures, languages and customs. At the beginning of the twentieth century, four-fifths of Catholics lived in Europe.[4] As the twenty-first century appears on the horizon, the proportion is virtually inverted, with only a quarter in Europe, with the rest spread over Latin America, where nearly half the world's Catholics live, the Caribbean, North America, Asia and Africa.[5] On the eve of Vatican II, though most Catholics were still to be found in Europe, many had already noticed the dramatic change that was taking place. The review *Fêtes et Saisons* entitled its special number for the opening of the Council *L'Eglise aux cents visages*, 'The Church with a Hundred Faces'. Diversity, not uniformity, is now the mark of the church, together with its rapid de-Westernization and de-Europeanization.

It is natural, given these new conditions, that the particular churches should have assumed an unheard-of autonomy and developed their own means of communication, exchange, collaboration and communion at national level, through bishops' conferences, national councils of lay people, national councils of priests, deacons, religious, or on a continental scale, with the links between conferences, councils and other bodies. CELAM (the Episcopal Conference of Latin America) had actually been created before the Council, in 1955, but it grew in consistency and capacity for action during the years the Council met. At the same time, the African episcopate created its own linking authority, forming itself into groups of countries sharing the common languages of French or English. In 1969 these regional conferences created a single body, SECAM (Symposium of Episcopal Conferences of Africa and Madagascar). The same year, Paul VI, on his first journey to Africa (31 July to 2 August), greeted the African bishops on his arrival with the words:

> We have no other desire than to foster what you already are: Christians and Africans. Hence we wish our presence among you to have the significance of a recognition of your maturity and of a desire to show you how that communion which unites us does not suffocate, but rather nourishes the originality of your personal, ecclesial and even civil personality.[6]

He went on:

> . . . the expression, that is, the language and mode of manifesting the faith, may be manifold; hence it may be original, suited to the tongue, the style, the character, the genius and the culture of the one who professes the one Faith. From this point of view, a certain pluralism is not only legitimate, it is desirable. An adaptation of the Christian faith in the fields of pastoral, ritual, didactic and spiritual activities is a living example of this. And in this sense you may, and indeed must, have an African Christianity.[7]

Today one has the impression that the conciliar experience, felt as a joyful and promising spring by the churches of the periphery, set free to live, build and express their ecclesial journey, in an inculturated fashion and in response to the huge challenges of their communities and peoples, was felt differently by many of the old Christendoms of Europe. This 'disenchantment' came out very clearly in the 'Dossier on the Faith' produced by Cardinal Ratzinger on the eve of the 1985 Extraordinary Synod, twenty years after the end of Vatican II, whose pessimistic, not to say bitter, tone contrasted with the hope-filled way the post-conciliar period was experienced at the time of Medellín and Puebla in Latin America:

> It is undeniable that these twenty years have been clearly unfavourable for the Catholic Church. The results that followed the Council seem cruelly opposed to the views of all, beginning with those of Pope John XXIII, then those of Paul VI. The Pope and the Council Fathers hoped for a new Catholic unity, and instead of this there has been a dissension that, in the words of Paul VI, has seemed to move from self-criticism to self-destruction. A new enthusiasm was hoped for, and yet it has ended in tedium and discouragement. We hoped for a leap forward, and instead of that, we have had a process of progressive decadence, which has taken place largely under the banner of a supposed 'spirit of the Council' and has, in this way, discredited it.[8]

Examining the future of particular churches, then, depends very much on the point of view one adopts: whether on the side of the pastorally and spiritually positive experience of the particular churches, local or continental, which have found their own face, evolved their own journey and their own magisterium; or on the side of the Roman centre, the source of contradictory signs of acceptance of these new ecclesial realities and even of suspicion, warning and revocation.

Hesitations along the way

After the end of Vatican II, as a development of the rediscovered collegiality of bishops, the first Synod of Bishops met in Rome in 1967. At the same time Pope Paul VI published two encyclicals, *Sacerdotalis coelibatus* (1967) and *Humanae vitae* (1968), on subjects which had been withdrawn from conciliar debate and not made the subject of synodal consultation: the ordination of married men and birth control. This pontifical decision sat uneasily with the post-conciliar climate and the encyclicals – particularly *Humanae vitae* – had a stormy reception.

Cardinal Eduardo Pironio, three times secretary of CELAM and then its president, intervened in the Synod of 1969 to express his disquiet and put forward a view of the exercise of primacy in which the pope would not be the sole centre of unity, while the bishops would represent diversity; the college of bishops united with the pope would be the principle of unity. The bishop represents the local church in which the universal church resides. The Roman Pontiff should be the defender of legitimate diversity and should prevent attempts to absorb the local churches.[9]

The harsh criticism by Cardinal Leo Joseph Suenens of the way in which he saw the collegiality of bishops and their joint responsibility for the whole church being eroded by the exercise of primatial power, which was failing to take account of the rest of the episcopal college, as had happened in the case of the two encyclicals, led Paul VI to include a debate on the presbyteral ministry, including the admission of married men to the priesthood, in the 1971 Synod (on the subject of justice); to give the Synod a secretariat of fifteen members, twelve of whom were elected by the bishops themselves; and to suspend the issuing of any more encyclicals for the remaining nine years of his papacy.

So on the eightieth anniversary of *Rerum novarum*, in 1971, Paul VI sent an apostolic letter, *Octogesima adveniens*, instead of an encyclical, to the president of the Justice and Peace Commission, Cardinal Le Roy. Its importance for the social teaching of the church was no less on that account. At the end of the Synod on Evangelization (1974), Paul VI issued an 'apostolic exhortation', *Evangelii nuntiandi* (1975), in which he summed up the most significant contributions from the bishops of the different continents, thereby overcoming the rejection by the synod members of the *Relatio finalis* presented by the then cardinal of Cracow, Karol Wojtyla. Paul VI made a point of stating that he had produced *Evangelii nuntiandi* 'because this was requested of us by the synod Fathers themselves. Effectively, at the close of this memorable Assembly, they decided to entrust to the Pastor of the Universal Church, with great confidence and simplicity, the fruit of all their labours, declaring that they looked to the Pope for a new impulse, one capable of arousing, in a Church still borne along by the strength and indwelling power of Pentecost, a new era of evangelization' (*EN* 2). Even presented as a humble apostolic exhortation, written at the request of the bishops, *Evangelii nuntiandi* has gone down in history as, alongside *Populorum progressio*, the most important text of Paul VI's magisterium.

Present-day practice has shown itself far from Paul VI's scrupulous care not to dim the exercise of collegiality or diminish the role of bishops and their leadership of local churches in their legitimate diversity. Even the most important piece of recent legislation, the new Code of Canon Law, promulgated in 1983, was not submitted for final approval or scrutiny by a representative body of bishops such as an Extraordinary Synod. In the same way, the *Catechsim of the Catholic Church*, published in 1992, was not subjected to the doctrinal and pastoral approval of a synodal assembly.

Equally in recent years Roman encyclicals and other documents have multiplied, even on subjects that required the resources of previous, more collegial discussion and composition, since they profoundly affect the life of particular churches in the exercise of their pastoral responsibilities as well as local churches in their exercise of episcopal collegiality. So the more recent documents have included one on the ministries carried out by lay people,[10] one setting out rules governing bishops' conferences,[11] and one legislating on diocesan synods.[12]

In the 'Instruction on certain questions concerning the collaboration of the lay faithful in the sacred ministry of priests', signed by representatives of six Roman Congregations and two Pontifical Councils, the title itself indicates the angle from which the subject is approached. The central focus is on the priestly ministry and the collaboration the faithful can bring to this, not on the rich diversity of new lay ministries, with their own worth and proper place in the life of the church deriving from the baptismal and ministerial calling of all Christians. This diversity of new ministries sustaining the life of the churches of the Third World, in basic church communities and pastoral centres, is one of the most glowing aspects of ecclesial experience over the past three decades.[13] In the document, many of these ministries are seen simply as a response to the shortage of priests and therefore as 'passing solutions' and ones ordained 'to a specific pastoral priority for the promotion of vocations to the sacrament of orders'.[14]

In the *Motu proprio* on bishops' conferences, instead of recognizing their necessity and value, regulations are introduced that are so demanding as to make their normal functioning, as part of the magisterium, virtually impossible. The document foresees that 'if doctrinal declarations made by a Conference are approved unanimously by the Bishops, they may be published in the name of the particular Conference, and the faithful should adhere in a spirit of religious obedience to that authentic magisterium of these Bishops, which must always be in communion with the Head of the College of Bishops, the Roman Pontiff. However, if such unanimity should not prevail, a qualified majority of the Bishops cannot publish the eventual declaration as the genuine magisterium of the Conference, to which all the faithful of the territory should adhere, unless such a document approved only by a qualified majority obtains the *recognitio* of the Apostolic See.'[15] As such unanimity has never been achieved, even in votes at ecumenical councils, the practical result is that the whole doctrinal magisterium of bishops' conferences has to depend on previous verification and approbation from Rome. The danger is that particular churches will be deprived of the rich magisterium of recent years and a dangerous disequilibrium will come about, leading to the atrophy of the local churches, which are far closer to emerging challenges. The temptation is to pursue a uniformity incapable of taking account of today's cultural diversity, abandoning recognition of the right for doctrinal expression to be couched in different languages and accents while safeguarding unity in essentials.

By its prescription that 'no body of the Episcopal Conference, with the exception of its plenary session, has the power to carry out acts of authentic magisterium',[16] conferences have been deprived of the capacity to delegate to their other bodies, such as the presidency, pastoral commissions or permanent council the ability to intervene in the intervals between plenary sessions. In countries that cover a vast territorial extent and have many dioceses, this restriction can introduce an element of paralysis, reducing the capacity of the conference to act in moments of crisis or serious situations.

Another collegial body that is suffering significant erosion is the synod of bishops. Synods seem to have reached their peak with the Synod on Justice in 1971. In the 1974 Synod on Evangelization the impasse brought about by the rejection of the *Relatio finalis* meant that the synod fathers abandoned publication of their own conclusions as a document carrying the full authority of the synodal assembly, but instead sent them to the pope. From that point on, the synodal assemblies lost their voice, with their conclusions reduced to suggestions made to the pope for him, later, to organize and publish as an apostolic exhortation.

On the pretext that they were consultative and not decision-making bodies, the synodal assemblies lost the capacity to produce their own agenda of the most pressing questions for the life of the church and to serve as a necessary counterweight to a Roman centralizing tendency that, limited by the Council, was being reimposed with redoubled force. Synods also lost the capacity to regulate themselves as an assembly: they had no part in preparing the *Lineamenta*, a minimal one in producing the *Instrumentum Laboris*, and absolutely none in choosing the members of the different bodies and commissions, all of whom were nominated by the pope. The growth in the number of members nominated *ex officio* meant that representatives of particular churches became a minority.

A practical example of this is the recent Synod for America, held in Rome from 16 November to 12 December 1997. Of its 297 participants, just 136 were bishops elected directly by their bishops' conferences. The majority, that is the other 161 participants, were either *ex officio* members or nominated by the pope, with the exception of the six major superiors elected by their peers. The criterion laid down by Rome for the choice of bishops falsified the representativeness of the episcopates, giving greater weight to small churches and drastically reducing the presence of the larger ones: the Dominican Republic, with nine bishoprics, elected three (one out of three); Brazil, with 256, elected fifteen (one out of seventeen).

This imbalance was even more marked among the *auditores* and *auditrixes*, all selected and nominated by the pope: Paraguay, Cuba and Mexico had two each, Colombia three, Canada four, the United States thirteen, and Brazil just one, a woman not known to the bishops' conference, which had not at any time been consulted or asked to put names forward. This imbalance provoked a challenge from the National Conference of Brazilian Bishops about the criteria employed and the obvious marginalization of the Brazilian church, with its one representative against thirteen for the United States, despite the fact that Brazil has twice as many baptized as the United States and the greatest number on the continent. In an assembly predominantly masculine and clerical, the *auditores* and *auditrixes* could have opened a window on the lay world, that of women in particular, especially in trying to outline the challenges and tasks for the church in the third millennium. Yet there were just twenty lay people (34.5%) compared to thirty-eight (65.5%) religious (of both sexes) or diocesan priests and deacons. There were eighteen women (31%) to forty men (69%), while in the synodal assembly as a whole their percentage dropped to 6.06. Even this proportion was a marked improvement on the total absence of women from the preparatory phases and first and second sessions of Vatican II, but totally insufficient in relation to the acceleration of history in the last few decades and as a sign of recognition of the central role women have taken on in the life of the church, let alone of the equal dignity and responsibility in the church with which they are invested through the sacrament of baptism.

The contrast between the Synod for America and the General Conferences of the Latin American episcopate held in Medellín (1968), Puebla (1979) and Santo Domino (1992) could not be clearer. The course of Vatican II gave rise to many dreams, one of which was that collegiality of bishops would find practical forms of expression, both on the level of particular churches, by means of episcopal conferences, and on the level of the universal church, through a collegial body working closely with the pope, without depriving him of the prerogatives of the Petrine primacy. A large number of the bishops also envisaged a synodal body with a decision-making character like that of general councils. In practice, Paul VI instituted the Synod as a personal consultative agency of the pope. Nevertheless, the dream of broad decision-making episcopal assemblies, even if it failed to take root at the centre, finally took concrete form on the periphery, in the Second General Conference of Latin American Bishops held at Medellín in 1968. At the end of the conference Paul VI, speaking by telephone to one of its presidents, Cardinal Andrea Samoré, agreed that the Fathers present could take the conclusions they agreed back to each particular church and publish them, subject only to later corrections suggested by the Roman Curia. In the event, some minor corrections were made and the official text of the conclusions was approved two months later by the pope, but the original version of the Medellín 'Conclusions' is still being reprinted in many countries. The two following conferences, in Puebla and Santo Domingo, kept their deliberative character, even though at Santo Domingo enormous pressure from Rome was put on the assembly not to approve a Final Document but simply to address a 'Message' to the people of Latin America and send its conclusions, in the form of suggestions, for subsequent drafting in a pontifical document addressed to Latin America. So a whole continent was to renounce its own magisterium, in communion with the See of Peter but with its own autonomy and accepting its own ecclesial and pastoral responsibility.

Many have seen the recent Synod for America as the means of putting a full stop to this other way of experiencing and practising synodality in the church, making decisions and making its own – often prophetic and courageous – voice heard in the universal concert of the church, as it was at Medellín.

Particular churches and the future of ecumenism

The value of particular churches and the conciliarity (synodality) of the church lies at the heart of the Orthodox tradition; the local assembly is an element that was revalued by the Protestant Reformation, given lively expression in the Congregationalist churches and taken to extremes by the Baptists. The reforms of Vatican II went back to some of these elements, emphasizing the importance of the local church and giving greater importance to collegial elements in the life of the Catholic Church. These are central features in ecumenical dialogue and drawing-together and communion among the Christian churches. John Paul II noted this in *Ut unum sint:* 'When the Catholic Church affirms that the function of the Bishop of Rome corresponds to the will of Christ, it does not separate this function from the mission entrusted to the bishops as a whole, who are also "vicars or legates of Christ" (LG 27). The Bishops of Rome belongs to their "college", and they are his brothers in ministry.'[17]

With ears and heart open to the plea from other churches to find a new way of exercising the Petrine primacy, the Pope replies that this is 'an immense task which we cannot refuse, but which I cannot accomplish alone'. He adds: 'The Holy Spirit gives us his light and enlightens all the pastors and theologians of our Churches, so that we may be able to discover, evidently together, the forms through which this ministry can carry out a service of love recognized by one and all.'[18]

André Scrima, the observer from the Orthodox Patriarchate of Constantinople as personal envoy from Athenagoras to Vatican II, observed at the end of the Council that 'the basic thesis of the ecclesial orientations of the Constitution [*Lumen Gentium*] is the assimilation (doctrinal and pastoral) of interdependence between the papacy and the episcopacy'.[19] This observation could be translated in terms of the relationship between the particular church of Rome and its primacy and other particular churches, carried out in the bosom of collegiality and communion among the churches and between them and the See of Rome.

The opening made by John Paul II in *Ut unum sint* received a nuanced response from the Anglican Church but has not yet provoked the in-depth debate it solicited. The main problem would seem to lie in the rather unsatisfactory form taken, for the present, by the relationship between exercise of the papal primacy and collegiality of bishops, between the See of Rome and the local churches and between this same See of Rome and bishops' conferences, which indicates a degree of disrespect for local autonomies and the responsibilities proper to particular churches and their expressions of communion and collegiality at regional, national and even continental level.[20]

CEBs: lack of juridical institutional recognition

Basic ecclesial communities (CEBs), precious fruits of the ecclesial revolution brought about by Vatican II, were explicitly recommended by Medellín as the place in which Christians gained their experience of community:

> So the basic Christian community is the first and fundamental ecclesial nucleus, which should, on its own level, be responsible for enriching and expanding faith, and also for the worship in which faith is expressed. It is, therefore, the initial cell of the church structure and focus of evangelization; it is also now a primordial factor in human promotion and development (Med. 15.10).

They were later recognized by *Evangelii nuntiandi* (1975) 'as a setting for evangelization, to the benefit of wider communities, especially the particular churches [. . . and a source] of hope for the universal church'. However, they received no recognition in the new Code of Canon Law, in which the basic church unit recognized juridically is still the parish. The basic communities, which are the life of the church at its roots through the wealth of their ministries, services and evangelizing efforts, simply do not exist for the legal framework of the church.

Is it better that they should stay this way, with a minimum of institutionalization and a maximum of prophecy, or should they find the stability and acceptance they merit as a structural element in the life of the church?

Ways forward for the future

Going back to the initial question of the future of particular churches, let us summarize the encouraging elements present in the individual and inculturated ways taken by particular churches, ways in which they have become stronger at the grassroots through a community life of pastoral endeavour and service and have inserted themselves into a rich web of relationships giving them a voice in episcopal conferences and in ecumenical communion with other Christian churches. We also need to point out the difficulties enumerated above, but above all we must see the future as a path to be marked out with courage and boldness, trusting in the Holy Spirit, which guides and inspires the church. Some of these tasks and wishes are:

1. The mechanisms of sharing and community should be strengthened at all levels of church life: CEBs, parishes, pastoral regions within dioceses, local churches and churches linked on a continental level or reunited in universal synods.

2. Baptism should be re-evaluated as the founding sacrament, which calls every Christian to develop her or his vocation in ecclesial ministries and services aimed at promoting evangelization and building church community, together with commitments in the world to justice, peace and the integrity of creation.

3. Because of this view of the church as the people of the baptized, channels of participation and decision-making should be devised within communities, pastoral parish councils and diocesan pastoral councils by which the whole church, in the wealth of its ministries for men and women, can be represented.

4. Diocesan synods or less formal and juridical diocesan assemblies (with representatives from basic communities, parishes, pastoral centres, special interest groups, Bible-study circles, catechetical teams, ministers of the eucharist and other sacraments, and any others who serve the community) should become the principal forum for taking decisions, together with the deacons, priests and bishop of the diocese, on its pastoral objectives and priorities.

5. Synods of Bishops should mature in the direction of greater co-

responsibility with the Bishop of Rome in the government of the universal church, adding elements of initiative and decision-making to their consultative function.

6. There should be a continued deepening of the process of liberating inculturation, taking cultural dimensions with socio-economic and political ones. In particular, in countries with indigenous majorities (Guatemala, Bolivia) or significant minorities (Mexico, Peru, Ecuador), the indigenous face of the church should be allowed to shine forth, as should its African-American face in places with a significant African presence.

7. Local churches should not be kept on the margins in the choice of their pastors, but ways for them to participate should be encouraged, always in combination with their bishops' conferences, the Congregation of Bishops, and the Bishop of Rome.

8. The foregoing proposals should be carried forward in a framework of ecumenical concern and attention, in the desire to intensify communion and strengthen unity among the Christian churches.

9. Finally, they should be adopted in a deep desire for fraternal and respectful dialogue with all other religious and humanist traditions, in the interest of being of greater service to men and women today in their quest for justice and peace and the means to overcome poverty, inequalities and conflicts.

Translated by Paul Burns

Notes

1. Cf. Leónidas Proaño, *Creo en el hombre y en la comunidad – Autobiografía*, Quito[3] 1989; A. Bravo Muñoz, *El soñador se fue, pero su sueño queda*, Quito 1998.

2. Bravo Muñoz, *El soñador* (n.1), 404.

3. For the *status quaestionis* and a definition of the concepts of local churches and universal church (not to be confused with the 'local church' of Rome), cf. H. de Lubac, *Les Eglises particulières dans l'Eglise universelle*, Paris 1973. [Here the term 'local' church designates a diocese, while 'particular' church signifies wider groupings – regional, national, or continental – *Trans*.]

4. In 1990, out of a world population of 1.6 billion, 401,000,000 lived in Europe, of which 207,000,000 (51.7%) were Catholic, with just 63,000,000 in the other mainly Catholic part of the world, South (38,000,000) and Central (25,000,000) America: cf. *Bilan du monde* I, Paris 1958, 3.

5. In 1997, of the 1.04 billion Catholics in the world, 117,900,000 were in Africa (11.34%); 111,215,000 in Asia (10.69%); 286,902,000 in Europe (27.57%); 442,807,000 in Latin America (43.62%); 73,880,000 in North America (7.1%); 7,710,000 in Oceania (0.74%).

6. *Insegnamenti* (1996), cited in P. Hebblethwaite, *Paul VI, The First Modern Pope*, London 1993, 536 n.1.

7. Ibid., in Hebblethwaite, *Paul VI* (n. 6), 537 n. 2.

8. V. Messorio, *Rapporto sulla fede – Entrevista con il Cardinale Joseph Ratzinger,* Milan 1985, 27–8. For a Latin American reaction to the book, see J. O. Beozzo (ed.), *O Vaticano II e a Igreja Latino-americana,* Sao Paulo 1985. For a European study, see P. Hebblethwaite, *Synod Extraordinary – The Inside Story of the Rome Synod,* London 1986, 50–62: 'Ratzinger invites Trouble'.

9. 'The community of bishops with the Pope should not be understood as though the Pope was the only centre of unity, while bishops represented merely diversity. The college of bishops, united to the Pope, is itself a principle of unity. The bishop represents the particular church in which the universal Church dwells. The Roman pontiff is the defender of legitimate diversity to the extent that he favours the cultural diversity of the Churches and prevents the absorption of particular Churches' (Hebblethwaite, *Paul VI* [n. 6], 554).

10. 'Instruction concerning certain questions relating to the collaboration of the lay faithful in the sacred ministry of priests.' See *The Tablet,* 22 November 1997, 1514.

11. *Motu proprio – Apostolus Suos,* 'The Theological and Juridical Value of Episcopal Conferences', 23 July 1998. See *The Tablet,* 1 August 1998, 1012, and weekly editions of *Osservatore Romano,* 1 and 8 August 1998, for the press conference given by Cardinal Ratzinger.

12. Instruction on Diocesan Synods, issued by the Congregation for Bishops and the Congregation for the Evangelization of Peoples, Portuguese text in SEDOC 30, no. 264, September-October 1997, 201–21.

13. For a view on the question of ministries from the standpoint of the churches of Latin America see A. Parra, *Os ministérios na Igreja dos pobres,* Petrópolis 1991; A. J. de Almeida, *Teologia dos Ministérios Nã-Ordenados na America Latina,* Sao Paulo 1989.

14. 'Instruction . . . relating to collaboration of lay faithful . . .' (34 in Spanish edition).

15. Cardinal J. Ratzinger in *Osservatore Romano,* 1 and 8 August 1998. See n. 11 above. See *Apostolos Suos,* Complementary Norms . . ., art. 1, regulating n. 22 of the document.

16. Ibid., Complementary Norms . . ., arts. 2, 8.

17. John Paul II, *Ut unum sint,* n. 95.

18. Ibid., nn. 96, 95.

19. A. Scrima, 'Simple Reflections of an Orthodox on the Constitution', in G. Baraúna (ed.), *The Church of Vatican II,* London and New York 1965.

20. On this aspect see the documents of the international convention organized by the Department of Religious Studies of the Catholic University of Milan, 16 to 18 April 1998, in *Il Regno* 10, 1998, 344ff, and the reports by H. Legrand, 'Primato e Collegialità al Vaticano II', in *Il Regno* 13, 1998, 449–55; A. Acerbi, 'Per una nuova forma del ministerio petrino', ibid., 456–64. On the difficulties faced by one particular church and especially its bishops' conference, see J. O. Beozzo, *A Igreja do Brasil: de João XXIII a João Paulo II, de Medellín a Santo Domingo,* Petrópolis 1996, esp. ch. IV, 'Tensão e diálogo – as relacções entre a Santa Sé e a Igreja do Brasil', 207–304. (There is a French translation of this by I. Berten, *L'Eglise du Brésil dans la tourmente – La reprise en main d'une Églisel,* 1992.)

Contributors

SEÁN FREYNE is a member of the editorial board of *Concilium* and is Professor of Theology at Trinity College, Dublin. His biblical studies have been conducted at the Pontifical Biblical Institute, Rome, and Jerusalem, and at the Institute for Ancient Judaism of the University of Tübingen. He is the author of several books and many articles on various biblical topics. His research interests deal especially with the social and religious world of Galilee in the Second Temple period.

Address: 24, Charleville Road, Dublin 6, Ireland.

JOSEPH MOINGT was born in 1915 and became a Jesuit in 1939. He was Professor of Systematic Theology successively at the Jesuit Faculty of Lyons-Fourvière and then at the Catholic Institute of Paris, and now holds that post at the Jesuit Faculty of the Sèvres Centre in Paris. He has been editor of *Recherches de Science religieuse* since 1968. His most recent book is *L'homme qui venait de Dieu*, Paris 1993.

Address: 15 rue Monsieur, 75007 Paris, France.

JÜRGEN MOLTMANN was born in Hamburg in 1926 and is a member of the Evangelical Reformed Church of Germany. He studied at Göttingen, and then was Professor at the Kirchliche Hochschule, Wuppertal from 1958 to 1963, Professor of Systematic Theology at the University of Bonn from 1963 to 1967, and until his recent retirement Professor of Systematic Theology in the University of Tübingen. Among his many works are his famous trilogy *Theology of Hope* (1967), *The Crucified God* (1974) and *The Church in the Power of the Spirit* (1992), and his newly completed systematic theology: *The Trinity and the Kingdom of God* (1981), *God in Creation* (1985), *The Way of Jesus Christ* (1989), *The Spirit of Life* (1992) and *The Coming of God* (1996).

Address: Universität Tübingen, Evangelisch-Theologisches Seminar, Liebermeisterstrasse 12, D 72076 Tübingen, Germany.

FELIX WILFRED was born in Tamilnadu, India in 1948. He is professor in the School of Philosophy and Religious Thought, State University of Madras, India. He has taught, as visiting professor, in the universities of Nijmegen, Münster, Frankfurt am Main and Ateneo de Manila. He was also a member of the Vatican International Theological Commission. He has been president of the Indian Theological Association and Secretary of the Theological Commission of FABS. He is a member of the Board of Editors of *Concilium*. His researches and field-studies today cut across many disciplines in humanities and social sciences. Among his publications in the field of theology are: *From the Dusty Soil. Reinterpretation of Christianity* (1995); *Beyond Settled Foundations. The Journey of Indian Theology* (1993); *Sunset in the East? Asian Challenges and Christian Involvement* (1991); *Leave the Temple* (1992).

Address: University of Madras, Dept of Christian Studies, Chepauk, Madras, India.

REGINA AMNICHT QUINN lectures in theological ethics in the Catholic Faculty of the University of Tübingen. She wrote her dissertation on the theodicy question (*Von Lissabon bis Auschwitz. Zum Paradigmawechsel in der Theodizeefrage*, Fribourg 1992) and her Habilitationsschrift on the question of religion and sexuality (*Körperdiskurs, Religion und Sexualität. Überlegungen zur Neusituierung einer theologischen Anthropologie und Ethik der Geschlechter*).

Address: Humboldtstrasse 1, 60318 Frankfurt am Main, Germany.

DIETMAR MIETH was born in 1940 and studied theology, German and philosophy. He gained his doctorate in theology at Würzburg in 1968 and his Habilitation in theological ethics in Tübingen in 1974. He became Professor of Moral Theology in Fribourg, Switzerland in 1974 and Professor of Theological Ethics in Tübingen in 1981. His publications include *Die Einheit von vita activa und vita contemplativa*, Regensburg 1969; *Dichtung, Glaube und Moral*, Mainz 1976; *Epil und Ethik*, Tübingen 1976; *Moral und Erfahrung*, Fribourg CH[3] 1983; *Meister Eckhart* (which he edited), Munich[3] 1986; *Gotteserfahrung – Weltverantwortung*, Munich 1982; *Die neuen Tugenden*, Düsseldorf 1984; *Geburtenregelung*, Mainz 1990; *Schwangerschaftsabbruch*, Freiburg im Breisgau 1991; *Das gläserne Glück der Liebe*, Freiburg im Breisgau 1992; *Grundbegriffe der christlichen Ethik*, Paderborn 1992 (with J. P. Wils); *Religiöse Erfahrung, Historische Modelle in christlicher Tradition*, Munich 1992, which he edited with W. Haug; and *Moraltheologie im Abseits*,

Antwort auf die Enzyklika 'Veritatis Splendor', Freiburg im Breisgau ²1995, which he edited.

Address: Universität Tübingen Katholisch-Theologisches Seminar, Liebermeisterstrasse 12, 72076 Tübingen, Germany.

CHRISTOPH THEOBALD was born in Cologne in 1946 and became a Jesuit in the Province of France in 1978. He is Professor of Fundamental and Dogmatic Theology in the Theological Faculty of the Centre Sèvres, Paris, and editor of *Recherches de Science Religieuse*, to which he contributes a bulletin on systematic theology (God – Trinity). His works in the history of modern theology and systematic theology include *Maurice Blondel und das Problem der Modernität. Beitrag zu einer epistemologischen Standortbestimung zeitgenössischer Fundamentaltheologie*, Frankfurt 1988, and 'La foi trinitaire des chrétiens et l'énigme du lien social. Contribution au débat sur la "théologie politique"', in *Monothéisme et Trinité*, Brussels 1991.

Address: 15, rue Monsieur, 75007 Paris, France.

ELISABETH SCHÜSSLER FIORENZA, Krister Stendahl Professor of Scripture and Interpretation at Harvard University Divinity School, is an internationally recognized feminist theologian and biblical scholar. Her latest publications are *Jesus: Miriam's Child and Sophia's Prophet* and *Sharing Her Word. Feminist Biblical Interpretation in Context*. She is the founding co-editor of *The Journal of Feminist Studies in Religion* and of the Feminist Theology issue of *Concilium*.

Address: Harvard University, The Divinity School, 45 Francis Ave, Cambridge, MA 02138, USA.

ANGELA BERLIS is a university assistant in the Old Catholic Seminar in Bonn. She gained her doctorate in Nijmegen in 1998 and was ordained deacon in 1988, priest in 1966. Since 1966 she has been working as an honorary chaplain for Old Catholic students in Bonn. Her publications include: 'The Ordination of Women in the Old Catholic Church', *Affirming Catholicism* 20, 1995, 29–36; *Frauen im Prozess der Kirchwerdung. Eine historich-theologische Studie zur Anfangsphase des deutschen Altkatholizismus (1850–1950)*, Frankfurt, etc. 1998.

Address: Alt-Katholisches Seminar der Universität Bonn, Adenauerallee 33, D 56315 Bonn, Germany.

GIANCARLO COLLET was born the child of Italian immigrant workers in Brunnen, Switzerland in 1945. A lay theologian, he studied philosophy and theology in Lucerne and gained his doctorate in theology in Tübingen. For a long time he worked in Mexico and is now Professor of Mission in the Catholic Theological Faculty of the University of Münster. His publications include: *Das Missionsverständnis der Kirche in der gegenwärtigen Diskussion*, Mainz 1984; *Der Christus der Armen. Das Christuszeugnis der lateinamerikanischen Befreiungstheologen*, Freiburg, Basel and Vienna 1988 (which he edited), and *Theologien der Dritten Welt. EATWOT als Herausforderung westlicher Theologie und Kirche*, Immensee 1990.

Address: Am Wittkamp 4, 48351 Everswinkel, Germany.

MAUREEN JUNKER-KENNY, Head of the School of Hebrew, Biblical and Theological Studies in Trinity College, Dublin, teaches Practical Theology and Christian Ethics. Her research areas include F. Schleiermacher and foundations of theology in modernity, the communicative ethics of J. Habermas, and biomedical ethics.

Address: University of Dublin, School of Hebrew, Biblical and Theological Studies, Trinity College, Dublin 2, Ireland.

CHRISTIAN DUQUOC was born in Nantes in 1926 and ordained priest in 1953. He studied at the Dominican house in Leysse, France; the university of Fribourg, Switzerland; Le Saulchoir; and the École Biblique in Jerusalem. He has a diploma from the École Biblique and a doctorate in theology. He is director of the journal *Lumière et Vie*, and his publications include *Christologie* (2 vols), Paris 1972; *Jésus, homme libre*, Paris 1973; *Dieu différent*, Paris 1977; *Messianisme de Jésus et discrétion de Dieu*, Geneva 1984; *Provisional Churches*, London 1986; *Libération et Progressisme,* Paris 1987.

Address: 2 Place Gailleton, 69002 Lyon, France.

MIKLÓS TOMKA was born in 1941; he studied economics and sociology in Budapest, Leuven and Leiden, and taught in Budapest, where he is now Professor of the Sociology of Religion. He has also been a visiting professor in Bamberg and Innsbruck. A co-founder of the Hungarian Pastoral Institute (in 1989), he is also Director of the Hungarian Catholic Social Academy and head of the Hungarian Religious Research Centre (both also from the same year).

Address: H-1171 Budapest, Vávix u.4, Hungary.

KARL-JOSEF KUSCHEL was born in 1948. He studied German and theology at the universities of Bochum and Tübingen. He did his doctoral studies in Tübingen, where he was an academic assistant, and from 1981 to 1995 worked at the Institute for Ecumenical Research and Catholic Faculty there. He is now Professsor of Culture and Inter-Religious Dialogue in the University of Tübingen. As well as editing many works, he has written *Jesus in der deutschsprächigen Gegenwartsliteratur* (1978); *Heute noch knien? Über ein Bild von Edouard Manet* (1979); *Stellvertreter Christi? Der Papst in der zeitgenössischen Literatur* (1980); *Gottesbilder-Menschenbilder. Blicke durch die Literatur unserer Zeit* (1985); *Weil wir uns auf dieser Erde nicht ganz zu Hause fühlen. Zwölf Schriftsteller über Religion und Literatur* (1985); *Born Before all Time: The Dispute over Christ's Origin* (1982); *Laughter: A Theological Reflection* (1994); *Abraham: A Symbol of Hope for Jesus, Christians and Muslims* (1995); *Im Spiegel der Dichter* (1997); *Von Streit zum Wettstreit der Religionen. Lessing und die Herausforderung des Islam* (1998).

Address: Sandäckerstrasse 2, 72070 Tübingen, Germany.

JOSÉ OSCAR BEOZZO was born in Santa Adelia (SP), Brazil, in 1941, and ordained priest in the diocese of Lins in 1964. He studied philosophy in São Paulo, theology at the Gregorian in Rome, and sociology and social communication at the Catholic University of Louvain. He is executive secretary of CESEP (Ecumenical Centre for Services to Evangelization and Popular Education), a member of the executive board of CEHILA (Commission for Study of Church History in Latin America) and a lecturer at the theology faculty of São Paulo University. His publications include *Trabalho, crise e alternativas* (1995); *Igreja no Brasil: de Joào XXIII a Joào Paulo II* (1995); and, as editor for the Brazil area, *Historia do Concilio Vaticano II* (1995).

Address: Rua Oliveira Alves 164, São Paulo (SP) 04210–060, Brazil.

Concilium 1999/1

The editors wish to thank the great number of colleagues who contributed in a most helpful way to the final project of this issue:

R. Aguirre	Bilbao	Spain
J. J. Alemany	Madrid	Spain
M. Althaus-Reid	Edinburgh	Scotland
N. A. Ancic	Split	Croatia
A. Antoniazzi Belo	Horizonte	Brazil
E. Arens	Frankfurt	Germany
J. Argüello	Managua	Nicaragua
P. Baud	Pully	Switzerland
G. Baum	Montreal	Canada
T. Berger	Durham, NC	America
W. Beuken	Leuven	Belgium
A. Blijlevens	Heerlen	The Netherlands
J. Brosseder	Koningswinter	Germany
P. F. Carneiro de Andrade	Rio de Janeiro	Brazil
C. Carozzo	Genoa	Italy
P. de Clerck	Paris	France
A. M. Clifford	Pittsburgh	America
J. A. Coleman	Los Angeles	America
S. Copeland	Wisconsin	America
R. G. Cote	Ottowa	Canada
K. Derksen	Utrecht	The Netherlands
G. Dietrich	Madurai	India
M. Dumais	Rimouski	Canada
C. Duquoc	Lyon	France
E. Dussel	Coyoacán	Mexico
K. J. Egan	Notre Dame	America
F. Elizondo	Madrid	Spain
V. Elizondo	San Antonio	America
M. Fabri dos Anjos	Sao Paulo	Brazil
E. G. Farrugia	Rome	Italy
I. Fischer	Bonn	Germany
B. Forte	Naples	Italy
O. Fuchs	Geneva	Switzerland
R. Gibellini	Brescia	Italy
E. Green	Bari	Italy
M. C. Grey	Wiltshire	England
F. Haarsma	Nijmegen	The Netherlands
F. Houtart	Louvain-la-Neuve	France
M. E. Hunt	Silver Spring	America
B. van Iersel	Nijmegen	The Netherlands
W. Jeanrond	Lund	Sweden
M. Junker-Kenny	Dublin	Ireland

B. Kern	Mainz	Germany
U. King	Bristol	England
M. Klöckener	Fribourg	Switzerland
M. Lamberigts	Leuven	Belgium
A. Lampe	Chemutal-Quintana	Mexico
H. Laubach	Mainz	Germany
B. Lauret	Paris	France
H. Lepargneur	Sao Paulo	Brazil
S. McEvenue	Montreal	Canada
F. W. Menne	Münster	Germany
J. M. de Mesa	Quezon City	Philippines
N. Mette	Münster	Germany
J. B. Metz	Münster	Germany
H. Meyer-Wilmes	Nijmegen	The Netherlands
F. G. Morrisey	Ottowa	Canada
E. Pace	Paduc	Italy
R. Panikkar	Barcelona	Spain
P. Philibert	Notre Dame	America
A. Pieris	Gonawala-Kelaniya	Sri Lanka
J. Porter	Nashville	America
D. N. Power	Washington	America
J. H. Provost	Washington	America
J. Riches	Glasgow	Scotland
A. Rizzi	Fiesole	Italy
R. Ruether	Evanston	America
G. Ruggieri	Catania	Italy
P. Schotsmans	Leuven	Belgium
R. Schreiter	Chicago	America
S. Singles	Lyon	France
J. Sobrino	San Salvador	El Salvador
C. Soetens	Brussels	Belgium
J. M. Soskice	Cambridge	America
L. Sowle-Cahill	Chestnut Hill	America
H. Steinkamp	Münster	Germany
P. Suess	Sao Paulo	Brazil
E. Tamez	San José	Costa Rica
J. E. Thiel	Fairfield	America
B. Tierney	Ithaca	America
J. S. Ukpong	Harcourt	Nigeria
E. Uzukwu	Wani-Enegu	Nigeria
M. Vidal	Madrid	Spain
E. Wainwright	Banyo	Australia
J. T. Walsh	Gabarone	Botswana
J. Walton	New York	America
F. Wilfred	Madras	India
M. Wijlens	Münster	Germany

Concilium 1990-1999

1990

1 On the Threshold of the Third Millennium *The Concilium Foundation*
2 The Ethics of World Religions and Human Rights *Hans Küng and Jürgen Moltmann*
3 Asking and Thanking *Christian Duquoc and Casiano Floristan*
4 Collegiality put to the Test *James Provost and Knut Walf*
5 Coping with Failure *Norbert Greinacher and Norbert Mette*
6 1492-1992: The Voice of the Victims *Leonardo Boff and Virgil Elizondo*

1991

1 The Bible and Its Readers *Wim Beuken, Sean Freyne and Anton Weiler*
2 The Pastoral Care of the Sick *Mary Collins and David Power*
3 Aging *Lisa Sowle Cahill and Dietmar Mieth*
4 No Heaven without Earth *Johann Baptist Metz and Edward Schillebeeckx*
5 *Rerum Novarum*: 100 Years of Catholic Social Teaching *Gregory Baum and John Coleman*
6 The Special Nature of Women *Anne Carr and Elisabeth Schüssler Fiorenza*

1992

1 Towards the African Synod *Giuseppe Alberigo and Alphonse Ngindu Mushete*
2 The New Europe *Norbert Greinacher and Norbert Mette*
3 Fundamentalism as an Ecumenical Challenge *Hans Küng and Jürgen Moltmann*
4 Where is God? *Christian Duquoc and Casiano Floristan*
5 The Tabu of Democracy in the Church *James Provost and Knut Walf*
6 The Debate on Modernity *Claude Geffré and Jean-Pierre Jossua*

1993

1 Messianism through History *Wim Beuken and Anton Weiler*
2 Any Room for Christ in Asia? *Leonardo Boff and Virgil Elizondo*
3 The Spectre of Mass Death *David Power and Kabasele Lumbala*
4 Migrants and Refugees *Dietmar Mieth and Lisa Sowle Cahill*
5 Reincarnation or Resurrection? *Hermann Häring and Johann Baptist Metz*
6 Mass Media *John Coleman and Miklós Tomka*

1994

1 Violence against Women *Elisabeth Schüssler Fiorenza and Mary Shawn Copeland*
2 Christianity and Cultures *Norbert Greinacher and Norbert Mette*
3 Islam: A Challenge for Christianity *Hans Küng and Jürgen Moltmann*
4 Mysticism and the Institutional Crisis *Christian Duquoc and Gustavo Gutiérrez*
5 Catholic Identity *James Provost and Knut Walf*
6 Why Theology? *Claude Geffré and Werner Jeanrond*

CONCILIUM

The Theological Journal of the 1990s

Now available from Orbis Books

Founded in 1965 and published five times a year, *Concilium* is a world-wide journal of theology. Its editors and essayists encompass a veritable 'who's who' of theological scholars. Not only the greatest names in Catholic theology, but also exciting new voices from every part of the world, have written for this unique journal.

Concilium exists to promote theological discussion in the spirit of Vatican II, out of which it was born. It is a catholic journal in the widest sense: rooted firmly in the Catholic heritage, open to other Christian traditions and the world's faiths. Each issue of *Concilium* focusses on a theme of crucial importance and the widest possible concern for our time. With contributions from Asia, Africa, North and South America and Europe, *Concilium* truly reflects the multiple facets of the world church.

Now available from Orbis Books, *Concilium* will continue to focus theological debate and to challenge scholars and students alike.

Concilium Subscription Information - outside North America

Individual Annual Subscription (five issues): £25.00

Institution Annual Subscription (five issues): £35.00

Airmail subscriptions: add £10.00

Individual issues: £8.95 each

New subscribers please return this form:
for a two-year subscription, double the appropriate rate

(for individuals)   £25.00   (1/2 years)   . . . .

(for institutions)   £35.00   (1/2 years)   . . . .

Airmail postage
outside Europe +£10.00   (1/2 years)   . . . .

Total . . . .

I wish to subscribe for one/two years as an individual/institution
(delete as appropriate)

Name/Institution . . . .

Address . . . .

. . . .

. . . .

I enclose a cheque for . . . . payable to SCM Press Ltd

Please charge my Access/Visa/Mastercard no. . . . .

Signature . . . . .Expiry Date . . . .

Please return this form to:
SCM PRESS LTD 9 - 17 St Albans Place   London   N1 0NX